Early praise for *Build Websites with Hugo*

I loved learning Hugo by building a real site from the ground up. Well-thought-out exercises at the end of each chapter ensure you master the material. If you run a website or blog and want to make it simpler, faster, and more flexible, then you need to read this book.

➤ **Kieran Tully**
  Solution Architect, Mastercard

Absolute guide for getting started on Hugo, and for learning how to build your next amazing website. A must read for documentation experts and technical writers looking to add power to their documentation website.

➤ **Aleemullah Samiullah**
  Senior Engineering Specialist, Software AG

There are so many introductions and tutorials out there about bringing a website online with WordPress, but *Build Websites with Hugo* is the introduction you need to get going fast—without a lot of overhead. Brian gives you the tools to start crafting something and sparks your creativity, making you want to create a fast, stylish, static site with Hugo. By the end of this book, Hugo will go from being a stranger to being one of your best friends.

➤ **Dan Sarauer**
  Computer Support Supervisor, City of Eau Claire

Build Websites with Hugo

Fast Web Development with Markdown

Brian P. Hogan

The Pragmatic Bookshelf

Raleigh, North Carolina

Many of the designations used by manufacturers and sellers to distinguish their products are claimed as trademarks. Where those designations appear in this book, and The Pragmatic Programmers, LLC was aware of a trademark claim, the designations have been printed in initial capital letters or in all capitals. The Pragmatic Starter Kit, The Pragmatic Programmer, Pragmatic Programming, Pragmatic Bookshelf, PragProg and the linking *g* device are trademarks of The Pragmatic Programmers, LLC.

Every precaution was taken in the preparation of this book. However, the publisher assumes no responsibility for errors or omissions, or for damages that may result from the use of information (including program listings) contained herein.

Our Pragmatic books, screencasts, and audio books can help you and your team create better software and have more fun. Visit us at *https://pragprog.com*.

The team that produced this book includes:

Publisher: Andy Hunt
VP of Operations: Janet Furlow
Executive Editor: Dave Rankin
Development Editor: Tammy Coron
Copy Editor: Jasmine Kwityn
Indexing: Potomac Indexing, LLC
Layout: Gilson Graphics

For sales, volume licensing, and support, please contact *support@pragprog.com*.

For international rights, please contact *rights@pragprog.com*.

ISBN-13: 978-1-68050-726-3
Book version: P1.0—May 2020

Contents

Acknowledgments

First off, this book wouldn't be possible without Hugo itself, which is a result of the fantasic work of the Hugo team. Thank you Bjørn Erik Pedersen, Steve Francia, and all of the other amazing people who've contributed to Hugo. Thanks to your work, making things on the web is fun again, and I'm excited to share the joy that Hugo brings to everyone who reads this book.

Thank you Tammy Coron for editing this book and keeping me on track. And for asking some pretty great questions when I failed to explain some things.

Thank you Andy Hunt for publishing this book.

Thank you Dan Kacenjar, Greg Myers, Ryan Palo, Aleem Samiullah, Dan Sarauer, Kieran Tully, and Stephen Wolff, for reviewing the draft of this book and catching errors before the general public would have. I wrote this book in chunks, and many pieces got moved around. Your keen eyes caught many places where inconsistencies crept in. Without your help, readers would have gotten confused or stuck in more than a few places.

Thank you to my business associates Mitch Bullard, Jeff Carley, Kevin Gisi, Alex Henry, Jeff Holland, Chris Johnson, Jon Kinney, Nick LaMuro, Myles Steinhauser, Jessica Stodola, Charley Stran, Josh Swan, Erich Tesky, Mitchell Volk, Chris Warren, Mike Weber, and Andrew Vahey for your continued support.

Thank you Lisa and Ana for inspiring me. Thank you Carissa, for your love and support, and for all you do for our family.

Preface

Are you using a database to serve content that rarely changes? If you're using WordPress, Ghost, or other solutions for your content site, you probably are. Or at best, you've set up caching strategies to speed things up and reduce database calls.

Database-driven content management systems like WordPress let you define a common theme shared across your site, making it a breeze to publish new content. However, since most content doesn't change in real time, you're sacrificing speed and scalability for features that benefit content creators and developers instead of the people who want to read your content. And that additional complexity means you need more resources in production too: more servers to handle the traffic, standby database servers, a caching layer you have to manage, and more.

There's no better way to make a snappy content site than by serving static pages from a traditional web server or a content delivery network (CDN). But you don't have to give up the rapid development features you've come to expect. Static site generators, like Hugo,[1] give you a fantastic middle ground. You get the theming and content management features of a database-driven site without the bloat, security vulnerabilities, or complexities associated with caching.

Hugo gives you a framework for building a fast, organized content site using many of the skills you already have. You define your layouts in HTML and your content in Markdown. Hugo has built-in support for tagging, categorization, related content, multiple output formats, image optimization, and asset handling. While you're developing your site, Hugo gives you a web server for testing, and automatically refreshes your pages as you change them. When you're done building your site, Hugo generates a static site that you can upload to your web server.

---

1. https://gohugo.io

There are other static website generators available, like Jekyll[2] and Gatsby,[3] two popular and well-known choices. Hugo has a few benefits over those other choices. First, Hugo uses a single binary with no dependencies, which means you don't need a complex build chain or additional runtimes like Node or Ruby to get started or use its features. Unlike Jekyll, Hugo doesn't assume you're creating a blog. And unlike Gatsby, you don't need to learn React to build your themes or content; if you already know HTML and Markdown, you can be productive right away. Finally, Hugo is incredibly fast when it comes to building the site. It can generate thousands of pages quickly, which comes in handy if you're using Hugo to build something like a documentation website.

In this book, you'll use Hugo to build a personal portfolio site that you can use to showcase your skills and thoughts to the world. You'll build the basic skeleton, develop a custom theme, and use content templates to generate new pages quickly. You'll use internal and external data sources to embed content into your site, and render some of your content in JSON and RSS. You'll add a blog section with posts and integrate Disqus with your site, and then make your site searchable. While this isn't a web design book, you'll integrate modern CSS into the site, and use Hugo's asset management features to process styles, images, and scripts. Then you'll integrate Hugo with Node.js and Webpack for those situations where you need a little more flexibility. Finally, you'll explore deployment with Netlify,[4] cloud storage, and traditional web hosts so you can share your work with the world.

What's in This Book

Each chapter of the book covers a specific part of the development process with Hugo.

In Chapter 1, Kicking the Tires, on page 1, you'll build the home page and a few supporting pages, along with a skeleton layout.

Then, in Chapter 2, Building a Basic Theme, on page 15, you'll transform the layout into a custom theme for the site. You'll break things up into reusable pieces and put everything in its place.

In Chapter 3, Adding Content Sections, on page 25, you'll create the projects section of the site. You'll work with custom content types and build out more customized layouts for your new content type.

---

2. https://jekyllrb.com/
3. https://www.gatsbyjs.org/
4. https://www.netlify.com/

Then, you'll integrate data into the site in Chapter 4, Working with Data, on page 35. You'll leverage front matter from your docs, data from external files, and data from external sites. You will also render some of your content as JSON data.

In Chapter 5, Adding a Blog, on page 55, you'll use what you've learned so far to use Hugo to build a static blog. You'll create a content template for blog posts, create a custom layout to control how your posts display, and add support for commenting. You'll generate lists of posts, including a main list of posts in reverse chronological order, as well as lists for tags and categories.

In Chapter 6, Adding Search to Your Site, on page 79, you'll get search working with your site using a search index along with some client-side JavaScript.

Next, in Chapter 7, Managing Assets with Pipes, on page 91, you'll set up a proper asset pipeline so that you can manage your JavaScript and CSS files more easily. You'll switch to using Sass for your stylesheets and explore some of Hugo's built-in features for handling images. You'll also look at integrating Webpack with Hugo, and using npm to manage tasks that make building your site easier.

In Chapter 8, Deploying the Site, on page 109, you'll explore a few methods to move your site to production for the world to see. You'll deploy to Netlify, then look at deploying to Amazon S3, and finally, how to deploy to more traditional web servers.

Finally, you'll find Appendix 1, Migrating to Hugo, on page 123, which explores the process of what it takes to move an existing site to Hugo.

At the end of each chapter, you'll find a few additional exercises that will help cement your knowledge of the concepts.

What You Need

You'll need your trusty text editor and some experience building things for the web with HTML and CSS. This book doesn't go into much detail about those things and assumes you've built websites before. You won't use any CSS frameworks for the layout of your site, but you will use a small amount of modern CSS. The CSS you'll use in this book is intended to demonstrate concepts, not to substitute for careful and professional design. However, if you're an experienced web developer, you'll be able to see exactly where you can apply your existing knowledge as you build out your design.

Hugo runs on Windows, macOS, and various flavors of Linux and BSD operating systems, and it's a single binary file with no dependencies. You'll download and install Hugo in the first chapter. The examples of this book use Hugo version 0.68.3.

Because Hugo is a command-line tool, you should be comfortable using the command-line interface (CLI). You'll use the `hugo` command throughout the book to build your site, launch a development server, and generate files. If you want to get more comfortable with the CLI, you'll find *Small, Sharp Software Tools [Hog19]* helpful.

The examples in this book will show CLI commands for copying and moving files. These commands will work in the macOS and Linux terminals, and they will also work on Windows machines using the Windows Subsystem for Linux if you've configured that. Alternatively, you can use your graphical environment or text editor to manage and create files.

Additionally, some experience with JavaScript will be helpful when integrating search into the site.

Finally, in Chapter 5, Adding a Blog, on page 55 and Chapter 7, Managing Assets with Pipes, on page 91, you'll use Node.js[5] for some additional tooling. You should have Node.js installed on your system by following the official installation instructions for your platform.

Conventions

Throughout the book you'll see commands like this:

```
$ hugo new site portfolio
```

This is a command that you'll type at your command-line interface. The dollar sign indicates the prompt. You won't type that character.

You'll also see code listings, like this:

```
<div class="container">

</div>
```

Sometimes, you'll see highlighted sections when adding new lines of code, like this:

```
<div class="container">
➤   <header>
➤     <h1>{{ .Site.title }}</h1>
➤   </header>
</div>
```

---

5. https://nodejs.org

You'll find instructions on where to add the code to your project with each listing, along with details on what the code does.

Online Resources

The book's website[6] has links to submit errata for the book as well as the source code for the sites you'll build in this book. The downloadable source code is there as a reference and contains the site as it exists at the end of each chapter.

---

6. http://pragprog.com/book/bhhugo

CHAPTER 1

Kicking the Tires

The best way to get comfortable with Hugo is to start building something with it. Throughout this book, you'll use Hugo to build a portfolio site with a blog. In this chapter, you'll develop a basic understanding of Hugo, layouts, content, and configuration, which form the foundation for working with Hugo as you build a basic site.

But first, you need to install Hugo.

Installing Hugo

Hugo is available as a single binary. You can install Hugo two ways: using a package manager, or by downloading the binary manually and placing it in a global location so you can run it anywhere.

Hugo comes in two versions: a regular version and an extended version that has additional support for asset management, which you'll want in Chapter 7, Managing Assets with Pipes, on page 91.

Package managers are utilities that let you install and remove programs and utilities. Linux systems often have a built-in package manager. If you're running macOS, you can install the Homebrew[1] package manager. If you're using Windows, you can install Chocolatey.[2] Finally, Linux users can install Linuxbrew,[3] a version of Homebrew for Linux that offers more up-to-date packages than the package manager that comes with their system.

Installation via a package manager is the easiest method, although you might not always get the most recent version.

---

1.   https://brew.sh
2.   https://chocolatey.org
3.   https://docs.brew.sh/Homebrew-on-Linux

If you're using a Mac and you have Homebrew installed, you can install the extended version of Hugo with:

```
$ brew install hugo
```

On Windows, if you have Chocolatey installed, you can install Hugo with this command:

```
$ choco install -y hugo-extended
```

To install Hugo manually, find the extended version's binary for your operating system on the Releases page[4] on GitHub. For example, if you're on Windows, you're looking for a filename like hugo-extended-x.y.z-Windows-64bit.zip. Download the file.

Now that you've manually downloaded the file, you'll want to add it to your PATH environment variable, which your command-line interface uses to determine where it can find executable programs. That way you can execute it without specifying the full directory location.

On macOS or Linux, copy the executable to /usr/local/bin, which is already included in your PATH environment variable by default.

On Windows 10, create the directory C:\hugo\bin. Copy the hugo.exe file you extracted to C:\hugo\bin, and then add that folder to your PATH environment variable. To do this, use the Windows Search and type "environment". Choose the option for Edit Environment Variables for My Account. On the screen that appears, press the Environment Variables button, locate PATH in the System Variables section, and press the Edit button. Add c:\hugo\bin. Press OK to save the settings, and then press OK on the rest of the dialogs to close them.

Once Hugo is installed, run the hugo version command from your command-line interface to ensure that Hugo is available in any directory on your system, and that you've installed the extended version:

```
$ hugo version
Hugo Static Site Generator v0.68.3/extended darwin/amd64 BuildDate: unknown
```

The hugo command has several subcommands that you'll use as you build your site. You can see a list of all commands with hugo help.

Hugo is installed and ready. Let's use it to build a basic site.

---

4. https://github.com/gohugoio/hugo/releases

Creating Your Site

Hugo has a built-in command that generates a website project for you; this includes all of the files and directories you need to get started.

Execute the following command to tell Hugo to create a new site named portfolio:

```
$ hugo new site portfolio
```

This creates the portfolio directory, with the following files and directories within:

```
portfolio/
├── archetypes
│   └── default.md
├── config.toml
├── content
├── data
├── layouts
├── static
└── themes
```

Each of these directories has a specific purpose:

- The archetypes directory is where you place Markdown templates for various types of content. An "archetype" is an original model or pattern that you use as the basis for other things of the same type. Hugo uses the files in the archetypes folder as models when it generates new content pages. There's a default one that places a title and date in the file and sets the draft status to true. You'll create new ones later.

- The config.toml file holds configuration variables for your site that Hugo uses internally when constructing your pages, but you can also use values from this file in your themes. For example, you'll find the site's title in this file, and you can use that in your layout.

- The content directory holds all of the content for your site. You can organize your content in subdirectories like posts, projects, and videos. Each directory would then contain a collection of Markdown or HTML documents.

- The data directory holds data files in YAML, JSON, or TOML. You can load these data files and extract their data to populate lists or other aspects of your site.

- The layouts folder is where you define your site's look and feel.

- The static directory holds your CSS, JavaScript files, images, and any other assets that aren't generated by Hugo.

- The themes directory holds any themes you download or create. You can use the layouts folder to override or extend a theme you've downloaded.

In your terminal, switch to the newly created portfolio directory:

```
$ cd portfolio
```

Take a look at the site's configuration file. Open the config.toml file in your text editor. You'll see the following text:

```
baseURL = "http://example.org/"
languageCode = "en-us"
title = "My New Hugo Site"
```

This file is written in TOML,[5] a configuration format designed to be easy to read and modify. The default configuration file only has a handful of data, but you'll add more as you build out your site.

Hugo's internal functions use the baseURL value to build absolute URLs. If you have a domain name for your site, you should change this value to reflect that domain. In this book, you'll use relative URLs, so you can leave this value alone until you're ready to deploy your site to production.

The title value is where you'll store the site's title. You'll use this value in your layouts, so change it from its default value:

```
kicking_tires/portfolio/config.toml
baseURL = "http://example.org/"
languageCode = "en-us"
title = "Brian's Portfolio"
```

Save the file and exit the editor. You're ready to start working on the site itself.

Building the Home Page

A typical web page has a skeleton that looks like this:

```
<!DOCTYPE html>
<html lang="en-US">
  <head>
    <meta charset="utf-8">
    <title>Title</title>
  </head>
  <body>
    <!-- some content goes here -->
  </body>
</html>
```

---

5.   https://github.com/toml-lang/toml

Every time you create a page, you start with a skeleton such as this and then fill in the body section. Your site will likely have a lot more common elements like navigation, a banner, and a footer. As you build out your site, you end up duplicating all of this content on every page, which is difficult to manage if you do it by hand. That's why dynamic sites are so popular; they provide mechanisms to reduce duplication by separating the content from the layout.

In a Hugo site, you define *layouts* that contain this skeleton, so you can keep this boilerplate code in a central location. Your content pages contain only the content, and Hugo applies a layout based on the type of content.

Hugo needs a layout for the home page of your site, a layout for other content pages, and a layout that shows a list of pages, like an archive index or a product list. The following figure illustrates this relationship:

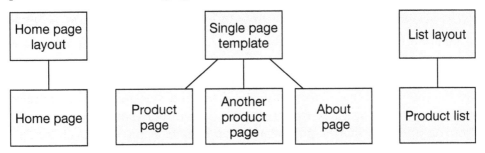

As you can see in the figure, the "home page" of the site has its own layout. The "Product list" page has a "list layout" associated with it. However, the two product pages and the "About" page all share a layout.

In this chapter, you'll create a layout for the home page and another layout for single pages, and they'll have nearly identical content. You'll build a layout for list pages in the next chapter.

Let's start with the home page layout. Hugo uses a separate layout for the home page because it assumes you'll want your home page to have a different look than other content pages. For example, your home page might contain a list of recent blog posts or articles, or show previews of other content. Or it might have a larger banner image than other pages. For now, you'll keep the home page simple.

Create the file layouts/index.html and add the following code, which defines an HTML skeleton for the home page:

```
kicking_tires/portfolio/layouts/index.html
<!DOCTYPE html>
<html lang="en-US">
  <head>
    <meta charset="utf-8">
    <title>{{ .Site.Title }}</title>
  </head>
  <body>

    <h1>{{ .Site.Title}}</h1>

    {{ .Content }}

  </body>
</html>
```

To pull in data and content, Hugo uses Go's http/templates library[6] in its layouts. While you don't need a deep understanding of how the templating language works, it's worth exploring when you want to build more complex templates.

In addition to the HTML code, there are some spots between double curly braces. This is how you define where content goes, and the content can come from many places. The {{ .Site.Title }} lines pull the title field out of the config.toml file you just edited and place it into the <title> and <h1> tags. The .Site prefix tells Hugo to get the value from the site's data rather than from the page's data. As you'll see shortly, pages have their own data that you can use.

The {{ .Content }} line displays the content for the page, which will come from an associated Markdown document in your site's content folder. Note that this doesn't use the .Site prefix, because this data is related to the page. When you're working with a Hugo layout, there's a "scope", or "context" that contains the data you want to access. The current context in a template is represented by the dot. In a Hugo layout, the context is set to the Page context, which looks something like this:

```
Context (.)
├── Site.
│   └── Title
├── Title
└── Content
```

For convenience, Hugo makes all of the site's data available in the Page context under the Site key. That's why you can do .Site.Title to get the site's title. To get the page title, you'd use .Title. There are many more pieces of data available to you within this context, and you'll use many of them later in the book.

---

6.   https://golang.org/pkg/text/template/

You've added the {{ .Content }} statement to the home page layout, but you're probably wondering where the content comes from. For the site's home page, Hugo will look for the content in a file named _index.md in the content directory. This special filename is how Hugo finds content for all index pages, like the home page and lists of content like tags, categories, or other collections you'll create.

Create the content/_index.md file and open it in your editor. You can place any valid Markdown content into this file. For this example, add a couple sentences and a list of what's on the site:

kicking_tires/portfolio/content/_index.md
```
This is my portfolio.

On this site, you'll find

* My biography
* My projects
* My résumé
```

After you've added your content, save the file.

Time to test things out. Hugo has a built-in development server that you can use to preview your site while you build it. Run the following command to start the server:

```
$ hugo server
```

Hugo builds your site and displays the following output in your console letting you know that the server is running:

```
...
Web Server is available at http://localhost:1313/ (bind address 127.0.0.1)
Press Ctrl+C to stop
```

Visit http://localhost:1313 in your web browser and you'll see your home page:

Brian's Portfolio

This is my portfolio.

On this site, you'll find

- My biography
- My projects
- My résumé

Use your browser's View Source feature and you'll see the layout and your content combined:

```
<!DOCTYPE html>
<html lang="en-US">
  <head>
    <meta name="generator" content="Hugo 0.68.3" />
    <script src="/livereload.js?port=1313&mindelay=10&v=2"
            data-no-instant defer></script>
    <meta charset="utf-8">
    <title>Brian&#39;s Portfolio</title>
  </head>
  <body>
    <h1>Brian&#39;s Portfolio</h1>
    <p>This is my portfolio.</p>
    <p>On this site, you&rsquo;ll find</p>
    <ul>
    <li>My biography</li>
    <li>My projects</li>
    <li>My re´sume´</li>
    </ul>
  </body>
</html>
```

Hugo's development server automatically reloads files when they change. Open the content/_index.md file in your text editor and make some changes to the content. When you save the file, the changes appear in your browser automatically. There's no need to install a separate server or browser extension. The single Hugo binary handles it all for you by injecting a little bit of JavaScript at the bottom of each page which handles reloading the page.

In your terminal, press CTRL+C to stop the Hugo server. You're ready to add another page to the site, but this time you will do it with Hugo's content generator.

Creating Content Using Archetypes

When you created content/_index.md, you created the file manually. You can tell Hugo to create content pages that contain placeholder content. This way, you never have to start with a blank slate when creating content. Hugo uses archetypes to define this default content.

The file archetypes/default.md—which was generated when you ran the hugo new site command—contains the following code:

kicking_tires/portfolio/archetypes/default.md
```
---
title: "{{ replace .Name "-" " " | title }}"
date: {{ .Date }}
draft: true
---
```

This is a Markdown file with YAML front matter and a little bit of templating code that will generate the title from the filename you specify, and fill in the date the file is generated. Hugo uses the front matter of each file when it generates pages. You'll dig into front matter a lot more in Populating Page Content Using Data in Front Matter, on page 36. Front matter isn't required in either content pages or archetypes, but you'll find it useful in many places as you build out your site. In this case, there's a draft field set to true. When Hugo generates pages, it will skip pages marked as drafts.

The hugo new command uses this file as a template to create a new Markdown file. Try it out. Create a new "About" page with this command:

```
$ hugo new about.md
/Users/brianhogan/portfolio/content/about.md created
```

This generates the file content/about.md. Open the file in your editor, and you'll see this code:

```
---
title: "About"
date: 2020-01-01T12:40:44-05:00
draft: true
---
```

The title is filled in, and the front matter also includes the date and time the file was created. It also has a draft status of true. Modify the draft status to false or remove the line entirely so that Hugo will generate this page. Then, below the front matter, add some additional content. When you're done, your file will look like this:

kicking_tires/portfolio/content/about.md
```
---
title: "About"
date: 2020-01-01T12:40:44-05:00
draft: false
---

This is my About page.
```

In order for Hugo to generate this page, you need another layout file. Remember that the layout you created, index.html, is only for the home page of the site. The "About" page you just created is an example of what Hugo calls a "single" page. As such, you need a "single page" layout to display it.

You can create different single page layouts for each content type. These get stored in subdirectories of the layouts directory. You're not going to do anything that complex yet. To create a default single page layout that every content page will use, store it in the layouts/_default directory. Create that directory now, either in your text editor or on the command line like this:

```
$ mkdir layouts/_default/
```

Now, create the file layouts/_default/single.html by copying the existing layouts/index.html file. Again, you can do this in your editor or the CLI:

```
$ cp layouts/index.html layouts/_default/single.html
```

Let's make a slight modification to this file; you'll have it display the page title in addition to the content. Open the single.html file in your editor and add the title like this:

kicking_tires/portfolio/layouts/_default/single.html
```
<body>
  <h1>{{ .Site.Title}}</h1>
➤ <h2>{{ .Title }}</h2>
  {{ .Content }}
</body>
```

Save the file and exit the editor. Then, start up the development server again:

```
$ hugo server
```

Visit http://localhost:1313/about and you'll see your new page:

Brian's Portfolio

About

This is my About page.

The site title, page title, and page content are all visible. The page title comes from the about.md file's front matter, while the site title comes from the config.toml file. This is a small example of how you can use data from various locations to build your pages.

Stop the Hugo server with CTRL+C. Let's explore what Hugo creates for you and look at a few options to control it.

Building and Exploring Hugo's Output

When you run hugo server, it generates your content in memory. To write Hugo's output to disk, run the hugo command with no options, like this:

```
$ hugo
...
                    | EN
+-------------------+----+
  Pages             | 5
  Paginator pages   | 0
  Non-page files    | 0
  Static files      | 0
  Processed images  | 0
  Aliases           | 0
  Sitemaps          | 1
  Cleaned           | 0

Total in 21 ms
```

This generates the pages for your site in a new directory named public. If you look at that directory's contents, you'll see these files and directories:

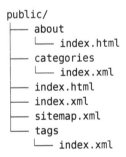

```
public/
├── about
│   └── index.html
├── categories
│   └── index.xml
├── index.html
├── index.xml
├── sitemap.xml
└── tags
    └── index.xml
```

Hugo has created the HTML files for your home page and the About page, as well as the file index.xml, which is an RSS feed for your site. It's also created a sitemap file, as well as RSS feeds for your site's tags and categories. You're not doing anything with those right now, so you can ignore them.

This public folder is your entire static site. To host it, you could upload the contents of the public folder to your web server, or upload it to your CDN. You'll explore how to put your site live in Chapter 8, Deploying the Site, on page 109.

Hugo doesn't clean up the public folder. If you were to remove some pages or rename them, you would need to delete the generated versions from the public folder as well. It's much easier to delete the entire public folder whenever you generate the site:

```
$ rm -r public && hugo
```

Alternatively, use Hugo's --cleanDestinationDir argument:

```
$ hugo --cleanDestinationDir
```

You can tell Hugo to minify the files it generates. This process removes whitespace characters, resulting in smaller file sizes that will make the site download faster for your visitors. To do this, use the --minify option:

```
$ hugo --cleanDestinationDir --minify
```

The public/index.html now looks something like this:

```
<!doctype html><html lang=en-us><head><meta name=generator
content="Hugo 0.68.3"><meta charset=utf-8><title>Brian's Portfolio</title>
</head><body><h1>Brian's Portfolio</h1><p>This is my portfolio.</p>
<p>On this site, you&rsquo;ll find</p><ul><li>My biography</li>
<li>My projects</li><li>My re´sume´</li></ul></body></html>
```

All the indentation and line breaks are removed. As a result, this file contains fewer bytes, which means it'll transfer faster when you eventually deploy the files to production.

Your Turn

Before moving on, try the following things to make sure you understand how page creation and content generation works:

1. Change the draft status of the About page's content back to true and regenerate the site with the hugo command, with no additional options. Notice that the about/index.html file still exists. Use the --cleanDestinationDir option and the about/index.html file will disappear. Set the draft status back to false again and rebuild the site to restore the file.

2. Create a "Résumé" page using hugo new resume.md. The generated title in the front matter will say "Resume". Open the content/resume.md file in your editor, update the generated title from "Resume" to "Résumé", and set the draft status to false. Fill in some content, and then run the development

web server. Navigate to http://localhost:1313/resume to view the page. The single page content template you created applies to this page as well.

3. Experiment with the default archetype. Change the draft state to false in the default archetype and generate a fourth page called contact.md. This new page will now have the draft state set to false. All future pages you create with the hugo new command will now have this status set.

Wrapping Up

You built a basic Hugo site, and you created a handful of content pages using Hugo's command-line interface. You've also defined the layout those content pages will use. However, you've got some duplicate code in your layout, which makes your site more difficult to maintain. In the next chapter, you'll extract your layout into a reusable theme and organize the code to reduce duplication.

CHAPTER 2

Building a Basic Theme

You've built your site, but you have two nearly identical layout files with a lot of duplicate code. Your site's layout is going to get more complex as you introduce additional content types, navigation, and styles, so it's time to start organizing things. So far, you've placed all of your layout files into your Hugo site's layouts directory, but Hugo has another mechanism for controlling how things look: *themes*.

There are many Hugo themes available that you can use, but instead of using one created by someone else, you're going to build your own. Many off-the-shelf themes are fairly complex with lots of features that take time to configure properly. It's best to understand how theming works before you dive into someone else's code.

A basic Hugo theme only needs these files:

```
layouts
├── _default
│       ├── list.html
│       └── single.html
└── index.html
```

This should look pretty familiar to you from the previous chapter. The index.html file is the home page of the site. The _default directory contains the default layouts applied to single content pages (single.html) and pages that display lists of content pages (list.html). However, as you'll discover in this chapter, there are some additional files you can create that will let you share code between files.

Let's get started with your theme.

Generating the Theme

You can make a theme by creating a new directory in the themes folder of your site, but Hugo has a built-in theme generator that creates everything you need for your theme. Execute this command from the root of your Hugo site to generate a new theme named basic:

```
$ hugo new theme basic
Creating theme at ...portfolio/themes/basic
```

This command creates the themes/basic directory and several subdirectories and files:

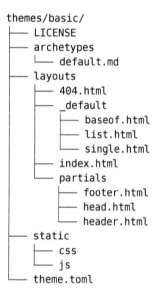

```
themes/basic/
├── LICENSE
├── archetypes
│   └── default.md
├── layouts
│   ├── 404.html
│   ├── _default
│   │   ├── baseof.html
│   │   ├── list.html
│   │   └── single.html
│   ├── index.html
│   └── partials
│       ├── footer.html
│       ├── head.html
│       └── header.html
├── static
│   ├── css
│   └── js
└── theme.toml
```

The theme has a place for its own archetypes, as well as directories to store the layout files and static assets like stylesheets, scripts, and images. Each theme has a license file so you can open source your theme if you choose, as well as a configuration file where you can store theme-specific configuration values.

Notice that there's already a layouts/_default directory with files for single page layouts and list page layouts. There's also a layouts/index.html file that serves as the home page layout. Those files don't have any content in them, though.

Move your existing layout files into this new theme. Move the layouts/index.html file to themes/basic/layouts/index.html, and then move layouts/_default/single.html to themes/basic/layouts/_default/single.html. You can do this quickly with these commands:

```
$ mv layouts/index.html themes/basic/layouts/index.html
$ mv layouts/_default/single.html themes/basic/layouts/_default/single.html
```

Before you can use the theme, you have to tell Hugo about it by adding a line to your site's configuration. Open config.toml and add the following line to the end:

```
basic_theme/portfolio/config.toml
baseURL = "http://example.org/"
languageCode = "en-us"
title = "Brian's Portfolio"
theme = "basic"
```

Save the file and run the server again:

```
hugo server
```

Visit http://localhost:1313 in your browser. Your home page still displays, which means your theme works. Once you know it works, stop the development server with Ctrl-c.

Now, let's break the theme up and reduce some duplication by taking advantage of Hugo's layout framework.

Using Content Blocks and Partials

Your home page layout and single page layout both contain the HTML skeleton. That skeleton is going to get a lot more complex once you add a header, footer, and navigation. Instead of duplicating that code in multiple places, Hugo provides a single place for you to put your skeleton so that all other layouts can build on it. When you created the theme, it generated it for you.

Locate the file themes/basic/layouts/_default/baseof.html and open it in your editor. You'll see this code:

```
<!DOCTYPE html>
<html>
    {{- partial "head.html" . -}}
    <body>
        {{- partial "header.html" . -}}
        <div id="content">
        {{- block "main" . }}{{- end }}
        </div>
        {{- partial "footer.html" . -}}
    </body>
</html>
```

This file will be the "base" of every other layout you'll create, hence its name. And instead of including the full skeleton, it's pulling in other files, or *partials*, which contain pieces of the layout. Placing common pieces in partials makes it easier for you to reuse these across different layouts, and it helps you think about parts of your site as components. The template generator also created these files, but it left them blank. Let's fill them in, one piece at a time.

The first partial listed in the baseof.html file is the head.html file, which you'll find in themes/basic/layouts/partials/head.html. This file will contain the code that would normally appear in the head section of a website. Open it in your editor.

Add the following code to the file to define the head element, with one meta tag that specifies the content type, another meta tag that specifies the viewport, so your page will scale properly on mobile devices, and finally, the title of the site:

```
basic_theme/portfolio/themes/basic/layouts/partials/head.html
<head>
  <meta charset="utf-8">
  <meta name="viewport" content="width=device-width, initial-scale=1">
  <title>{{ .Site.Title }}</title>
</head>
```

Save the file when you've made those changes.

The next partial reference is the header.html file, so open the file themes/basic/layouts/partials/header.html. This file will hold the header of your page. It's where you'll put the banner and navigation. Add the following code to add an HTML header section and a nav section with links to the root of the site and the static pages you created in the previous chapter:

```
basic_theme/portfolio/themes/basic/layouts/partials/header.html
<header>
  <h1>{{ .Site.Title }}</h1>
</header>

<nav>
  <a href="/">Home</a>
  <a href="/about">About</a>
  <a href="/resume">Résumé</a>
  <a href="/contact">Contact</a>
</nav>
```

Hugo has support for a more complex menu system, where you can configure your menu titles and destinations in your site's configuration file, but for small sites like this, it's less work to hard-code the URLs in the navigation. Since the navigation is in a partial, you only have to maintain it in a single file, so there's no advantage to doing it in a data-driven fashion like you would with a dynamic site.

Finally, create the footer of the site by opening themes/basic/layouts/_default/partials/footer.html, the last partial referenced in the baseof.html file. Add a footer element and a copyright date to the file with the following code:

basic_theme/portfolio/themes/basic/layouts/partials/footer.html

```
<footer>
  <small>Copyright {{now.Format "2006"}} Me.</small>
</footer>
```

You're using Go's date formatting to print out the current year. Go uses Mon Jan 2 15:04:05 MST 2006 as a reference time for its formatters. Instead of having to use special characters to parse out a current time, Go lets you use this reference time to format the specific dates and times. In this case, you only want the year, so you can use "2006" as the formatting string.

All of the partials for the base template are in place, but before moving on, let's look at the syntax for partials in the baseof.html file. Partials in the baseof.html template that Hugo generated for you look like this:

```
{{- partial "head.html" . -}}
```

Previously, when you've used those curly braces to inject the title, you used {{. But this code uses {{-. The dash suppresses whitespace characters in the output, such as spaces and newline characters. Placing a dash after the opening braces removes all whitespace in front of the expression, and placing the dash in front of the closing braces removes whitespace after the expression. In most cases, it's up to you whether or not you want to use them, but you'll often see dashes used to reduce the number of blank lines in the files Hugo generates.

In addition to the dashes, there's a dot after the name of the partial. The partial function takes a filename and a context for the data. In order to access data like the page title and content, you have to pass the context to the partial function, and a period means "the current context." Remember that the default context for a layout is the Page context, so when you pass the dot to the partial function, you're making the Page context available to the partial.

To use the new base template, replace the existing layouts you've used with code that defines a layout "block". In the baseof.html file, you'll find this line:

```
{{- block "main" . }}{{- end }}
```

This line looks for a block named "main" and pulls it in. Those blocks are what you'll define in your actual layout pages like index.html and single.html. Notice it's also passing the current context, so you'll be able to access it in the layout pages.

Define this block in your home page layout first. Open themes/basic/layouts/index.html and replace the contents with this code, which defines the main block:

`basic_theme/portfolio/themes/basic/layouts/index.html`

```
{{ define "main" }}

  {{ .Content }}

{{ end }}
```

When Hugo builds the site, it'll construct the home page by combining the content file (content/_index.md) with the layout file, which will then use the baseof file. The partials and content are all assembled, creating the full page.

The index.html layout only affects your site's home page, so modify the code in themes/basic/layouts/_default/single.html so the single page layout works the same way:

`basic_theme/portfolio/themes/basic/layouts/_default/single.html`

```
{{ define "main" }}

  <h2>{{ .Title }}</h2>

  {{ .Content }}

{{ end }}
```

This code looks just like the code in the home page layout, except you're also displaying the title of the page.

With the changes in place, make sure all your files are saved and then fire up the development server with hugo server. Visit http://localhost:1313 and test your pages. The home page displays with the current year displayed in the footer.

Brian's Portfolio

Home About Résumé Contact

This is my portfolio.

On this site, you'll find

- My biography
- My projects
- My résumé

Copyright 2020 Me.

Use the navbar you created to jump between pages to ensure they all work.

You now have a working theme that's organized and maintainable. Let's add some CSS to make it look nice.

Styling the Theme with CSS

In addition to layout files, themes contain images, scripts, and the stylesheets that control the visual aspects of the site, such as colors, fonts, and placement of content. These assets go in the static/ directory of your theme. You'll find both a css folder and js folder in your theme's static folder.

To style your site, you could bring in any number of CSS frameworks, but for this site, you'll build a very bare-bones layout by hand using plain CSS. Modern browsers have built-in support for newer CSS features like Flexbox[1] or CSS Grid, which makes it much less challenging to build a layout.

The theme you're going to build in this book won't win any design awards, but it will give you a place to start from and show you how to integrate CSS into your Hugo site.

Before diving into the CSS, let's add more structure to the layout so you can have more control over the width of the page. This will be helpful on larger devices. Modify the baseof file to wrap everything in a div with the class of container, and change the existing div tag around the main block to an HTML main sectioning tag. The main tag will make it easier for assistive technology to identify the site's main content, and the container div will let you control how wide the site is on larger monitors when you add the CSS:

```
basic_theme/portfolio/themes/basic/layouts/_default/baseof.html
<!DOCTYPE html>
<html>
    {{- partial "head.html" . -}}
    <body>
      <div class="container">
        {{- partial "header.html" . -}}
        <main>
        {{- block "main" . }}{{- end }}
        </main>
        {{- partial "footer.html" . -}}
      </div>
    </body>
</html>
```

Save the file.

---

1. https://www.w3.org/TR/css-flexbox-1/

Now, create the stylesheet itself. Since you're making a theme, create the file themes/basic/static/css/style.css.

In the file, add this code to define the width of the container:

basic_theme/portfolio/themes/basic/static/css/style.css
```
.container {
  margin: 0 auto;
  width: 80%;
}
```

Next, define the background and foreground colors for the navigation bar and footer of the site, and center the text in both:

basic_theme/portfolio/themes/basic/static/css/style.css
```
nav, footer {
  background-color: #333;
  color: #fff;
  text-align: center;
}
```

On small screens, the navigation elements will need to stack as a list; on larger screens, the navigation can be a long horizontal navigation bar. Add this code to style the navbar for both small and large screens:

basic_theme/portfolio/themes/basic/static/css/style.css
```
nav {
  display: flex;
  flex-direction: column;
}

nav > a {
  flex: 1;
  text-align: center;
  text-decoration: none;
  color: #fff;
}

@media only screen and (min-width: 768px) {
  nav { flex-direction: row; }
}
```

This code defines the nav element as a Flexbox region and defines the elements in the region to flow as a column. It then sets the anchor elements within the navbar as flex elements, evenly spaced apart. After that, it defines a color for each element and centers the text for each link. From there, using a media query targeting on larger screens, it redefines the flex-direction to align the contents as a row.

Finally, in the head.html partial, add a link tag to load a stylesheet named style.css, which will be located in the css directory:

```
basic_theme/portfolio/themes/basic/layouts/partials/head.html
<head>
  <meta charset="utf-8">
  <meta name="viewport" content="width=device-width, initial-scale=1">
  <title>{{ .Site.Title }}</title>
➤ <link rel="stylesheet" href="{{ "css/style.css" | relURL }}">
```

The relURL function creates site-root-relative link to the file instead of an absolute link that contains the site's domain name. For ease of development and deployment, you should use relative URLs whenever possible. When Hugo generates the site, it'll copy the contents of the themes/basic/static directory, including all subdirectories, into the public directory, so your CSS file will be located at /css/style.css.

Save the file and switch back to your browser. The styles are applied to the page and you have a basic theme. In Chapter 7, Managing Assets with Pipes, on page 91, you'll explore more things you can do with CSS.

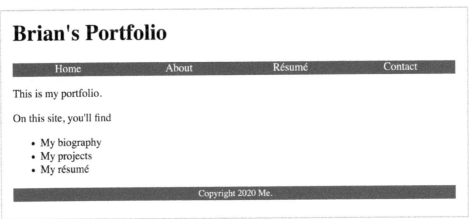

In this chapter, you kept the stylesheet in the static directory of the theme instead of in the static directory in your Hugo site. It's best to follow this convention and use your site's static directory for images or other assets that are specific to your site, and keep things that are specific to the theme within the theme's directory structure. When you generate your site, Hugo will grab files from both places and put them in the public directory. If you name files the same, the ones in your site's static directory will override the ones in the theme.

Your Turn

To solidify your understanding of how theming works in Hugo, try the following exercises:

1. Currently, the header partial contains the site's header and navigation. Use what you've learned about partials to move the navigation section into its own partial called nav.html.

2. Create a new theme named "bootstrap" using the theme generator. Create a layout using Bootstrap instead of your own custom CSS. Follow Bootstrap's documentation[2] to create your theme. To test it out, be sure to switch your site's theme in config.toml. Be sure to switch the theme back to basic before continuing on with the book.

3. Look at the Hugo theme gallery[3] and examine the source code for an existing theme you like. If you have Git installed, use Git to download the theme to your site and try it out. Many public themes have additional settings you'll have to configure, so explore the documentation for the theme you select.

Wrapping Up

You now know how to create a Hugo theme from scratch, using regular HTML and CSS, along with a small amount of Go's templating language. Your layouts are defined in a clear maintainable way, and you'll add more to your theme in the following chapters.

You're ready to look at Hugo's powerful content creation and management features.

---

2. https://getbootstrap.com/docs/4.1/getting-started/introduction/
3. https://themes.gohugo.io/

CHAPTER 3

Adding Content Sections

Hugo is designed to help you get your content in front of people quickly. Hugo has a few rules and conventions about how it handles collections of content, and understanding them will let you add and manage entire content sections to your site quickly.

In this chapter, you'll build a "projects" section of the site that showcases things you've accomplished. You'll create a custom layout for projects so they're visually distinct from the other pieces of your site, and you'll use Hugo's archetypes feature to create a content template so you can create new project pages quickly.

Let's start with that content template.

Creating a Project Archetype

In Creating Content Using Archetypes, on page 8, you learned about the default archetype that Hugo automatically includes when you generate a new site. When you created new pages, this archetype acted as a content template, filling in the YAML front matter for you. You can create more specific archetypes for other types of content and include whatever you'd like, including placeholder content.

Create the file archetypes/projects.md and open it in your editor. Add the following to the file, which defines not only front matter, but some placeholder content:

```
content_sections/portfolio/archetypes/projects.md
---
title: "{{ replace .Name "-" " " | title }}"
draft: false
---

![alt](//via.placeholder.com/640x150)

Description...
```

```
### Tech used

* item
* item
* item
```

The front matter is nearly identical to the content in the default archetype, which uses some Go template functions to generate the page name from the filename. But unlike the default archetype, you're adding some content to the body. You specified a placeholder image, a placeholder for the description, and a "Tech Used" section where you can list the various pieces of technology you used. Whenever you generate a new project, Hugo uses this file as the basis, and you can use the placeholder text here to quickly fill out your project's details.

Save the file and try it out. Create a new project page with the hugo new command:

```
$ hugo new projects/awesomeco.md
/Users/brianhogan/portfolio/content/projects/awesomeco.md created
```

This generates content/projects/awesomeco.md. The hugo new command creates files in the content directory, and since you prefixed the filename with projects/, Hugo looked for, and found, a projects archetype, which it used to create this file.

When you open the file, you'll see that Hugo used your new project archetype instead of the default:

content_sections/portfolio/content/projects/awesomeco.md
```
---
title: "Awesomeco"
draft: false
---

![alt](//via.placeholder.com/640x150)

Description...

### Tech used

* item
* item
* item
```

Replace the placeholder text with some details associated with the project. Save the file, start up the development server with hugo server, and visit http://localhost:1313/projects/awesomeco to view the project page as shown in the screenshot on page 27.

Stop the server and create another project page with the hugo new command:

```
$ hugo new projects/jabberwocky.md
```

This creates the file content/projects/jabberwocky.md. Start up the server again. You'll find this file at http://localhost:1313/projects/jabberwocky.

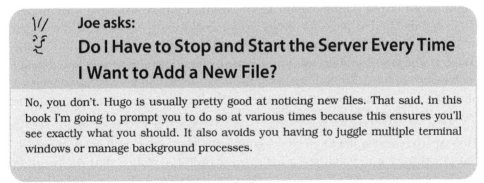

Joe asks:

Do I Have to Stop and Start the Server Every Time I Want to Add a New File?

No, you don't. Hugo is usually pretty good at noticing new files. That said, in this book I'm going to prompt you to do so at various times because this ensures you'll see exactly what you should. It also avoids you having to juggle multiple terminal windows or manage background processes.

You now have a fast way to generate pages that showcase your projects. All you have to do is generate a new page and fill in the details. Archetypes can be fantastic boilerplates that guide you as you create additional content.

Unfortunately, if you visited http://localhost:1313/projects, instead of a list of projects, you won't see anything at all. That's because you haven't defined a layout that displays lists. Let's do that now.

Creating the List Layout

Up until this point, you've only worked with individual pages, like the home page or a project page. You haven't done anything with lists of content yet. But if you're looking to show a list of tags, categories, or in this case, projects, you have to define a layout for those named list.html. When you generated the theme, Hugo placed a list layout in the themes/basic/layouts/_default directory, but it's blank. That's why you don't see anything when you visit http://local-host:1313/projects.

Let's define a default list template that will work for all list pages on the site. Open the file themes/basic/layouts/_default/list.html and add the following code to the file, which displays the title of the content page and builds a list of links to each content page:

content_sections/portfolio/themes/basic/layouts/_default/list.html

```
{{ define "main" }}

  <h2>{{ .Title }}</h2>
  <ul>
    {{ range .Pages }}
      <li><a href="{{ .RelPermalink }}">{{ .Title }}</a></li>
    {{ end }}
  </ul>

{{ end }}
```

The {{ range .Pages }} section is where the magic happens. The .Pages collection contains all of the pages related to the section you're working with. When Hugo builds the list page for Projects, for example, it collects all the pages within content/projects and makes those available in the .Pages variable in the context. The range function lets you iterate over the results so you can display each record in the collection. Inside of the range block, you access the properties of each page, as the context is now set to that specific page's context. In this case, you're displaying the site-relative URL and title of each page.

Fire up the development server again with hugo server and visit http://local-host:1313/projects, and you'll see a list of your projects. Notice that the heading on the page also shows "Projects". The .Title variable at the top of the layout file uses the content type's title:

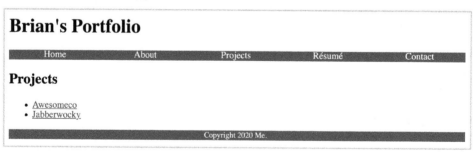

With this in place, add a Projects link to your main navigation so visitors can find that section. In the exercises at the end of Chapter 2, Building a Basic Theme, on page 15, you moved your navigation from the header partial to its

own nav partial. Open themes/basic/layouts/partials/nav.html and add the link to the /projects url:

```
content_sections/portfolio/themes/basic/layouts/partials/nav.html
<nav>
  <a href="/">Home</a>
  <a href="/about">About</a>
  <a href="/projects">Projects</a>
  <a href="/resume">Résumé</a>
  <a href="/contact">Contact</a>
</nav>
```

The default list layout you made is very generic. It's a good start and will serve you well when you add other content types to your site later. Let's create more specific layouts for projects so you can make project pages look a little different.

Creating More Specific Layouts

You'll often find that you'll want some pages or sections of your site to have slightly different themes or layouts. Let's make a specific layout for project pages that displays the list of projects in the sidebar of each project page so that visitors can navigate through projects easier. You'll use a similar approach to the one you just used to make the list of projects.

In the themes/basic/layouts folder, create a new folder named projects. You can do that on the command line like this:

```
$ mkdir themes/basic/layouts/projects/
```

Then, create the file themes/basic/layouts/projects/single.html. Add this code to define the main block with sections for the content and the project list:

```
content_sections/portfolio/themes/basic/layouts/projects/single.html
{{ define "main" }}
  <div class="project-container">
    <section class="project-list">
      <h2>Projects</h2>
    </section>

    <section class="project">
      <h2>{{ .Title }}</h2>

      {{ .Content }}
    </section>

  </div>
{{ end }}
```

In the project-list section, add the code to iterate over all of your projects and display a link to each page. Since you're not working with a collection in a list layout, you won't have access to a .Pages variable. Hugo provides a mechanism where you can access any content collection. The .Site.RegularPages variable gives you access to all of the pages in your site. You can whittle that down with the where function, which works similar to how a SQL statement works. For example, to find all of the Project pages, you'd write this statement:

```
{{ range (where .Site.RegularPages "Type" "in" "projects") }}
```

So, to display the list of all projects, add this code to the project_list section:

content_sections/portfolio/themes/basic/layouts/projects/single.html
```
<section class="project-list">
  <h2>Projects</h2>
➤ <ul>
➤   {{ range (where .Site.RegularPages "Type" "in" "projects") }}
➤     <li><a href="{{ .RelPermalink }}">{{ .Title }}</a></li>
➤   {{ end }}
➤ </ul>
</section>
```

You can sort the items too. If you'd like to order them by the most recent project first, use the .ByDate function and the .Reverse function like this:

```
range (where .Site.RegularPages "Type" "in" "projects").ByDate.Reverse
```

If you only wanted to display the most recent project, you could do this:

```
range first 1 (where .Site.RegularPages "Type" "in" "projects").ByDate.Reverse
```

This would be one way to showcase your most recent project on your site's home page. Note that even though you're only getting one element, you still treat it like a collection.

Start up the development server, switch back to your browser, and visit a project page. The list of projects shows up at the top of your page. Let's turn that project list into a sidebar with a little CSS.

Open themes/basic/static/css/style.css in your editor. Locate the media query that targets screens larger than 768 pixels wide, and add the following code to align the project list to the left of the screen in those situations:

content_sections/portfolio/themes/basic/static/css/style.css
```
@media only screen and (min-width: 768px) {
  nav { flex-direction: row; }

➤ .project-container { display: flex; }
➤
➤ .project-container .project-list { width: 20%; }
➤
➤ .project-container .project { flex: 1; }
}
```

The project info and the project list are contained in an element with the class project. Applying display: flex to that element makes the two child elements sit side by side. You then set the width of the project list section to 20%, and you set flex: 1 for the project_info section, which causes the element expands to fill the space. This gives you a nice two-column layout.

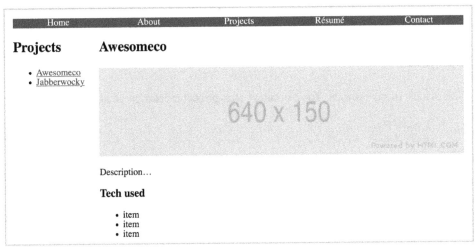

Before moving on, let's look at how to add Markdown content to the page that lists your projects.

Adding Content to List Pages

When you visit http://localhost:1313/projects,you see a list of projects and nothing else. Let's add some content to the page as well. To add content to list pages, you need to add an _index.md file to the folder associated with the content. This is similar to how you added content to your site's home page.

Create the file content/projects/_index.md. You can do this with the hugo command:

```
$ hugo new projects/_index.md
/Users/brianhogan/portfolio/content/projects/_index.md created
```

Open the file in your editor. It'll have the front matter filled in, and it'll also have the placeholder content, since it applied the projects.md archetype. Replace the content with some text that introduces your projects:

```
content_sections/portfolio/content/projects/_index.md
---
title: "Projects"
draft: false
---

This is a list of my projects. You can select each project to learn more about
each one.
```

The list template you created earlier doesn't display the content. Open themes/
basic/layouts/_default/list.html and add code to include the content into the layout:

content_sections/portfolio/themes/basic/layouts/_default/list.html
```
    <h2>{{ .Title }}</h2>
```
➤
```
    {{ .Content }}
```

Make sure both files are saved and view your project list to see the content:

Projects

This is a list of my projects. You can select each project to learn more about each one.

- Awesomeco
- Jabberwocky

With this in place, all list pages in your site support additional content, not
just your project list. However, all of those lists will look the same. Let's make
a layout for the project list next.

Customizing the Project List

Just like how you can create layouts for individual items in a content section,
you can control how the list for a content section looks with its own list layout.
The default list layout uses a bulleted list, but let's make a layout for projects
with a little more structure.

Create the file themes/basic/layouts/projects/list.html. Define the main block, bring in
the page title and the content section, and then iterate through the pages the
same way you did for the default list page, but use HTML sectioning elements
instead of a list:

content_sections/portfolio/themes/basic/layouts/projects/list.html
```
{{ define "main" }}

  <h2>{{ .Title }}</h2>

  {{ .Content }}

  <section class="projects">
    {{ range .Pages }}
    <section class="project">
      <h3><a href="{{ .RelPermalink }}">{{ .Title }}</a></h3>
    </section>
    {{ end }}
  </section>

{{ end }}
```

Save the file and view the projects list again to see the changes:

Projects

This is a list of my projects. You can select each project to learn more about each one.

Awesomeco

Jabberwocky

In Chapter 4, Working with Data, on page 35, you'll add more information about each project to this page, but for now this demonstrates that you can override the default layout for a content section.

Your Turn

1. Add the most recent project to the site's home page by modifying the index layout for the site.

2. Create a new type of content named "Presentations". Create the archetype, a new single page template, a list template, a couple of content pages, and wire it up to your navigation.

Wrapping Up

You've added a new Projects section to your site so you can show off your projects. Whenever you want to add a new project, you can generate a new content page with ease, thanks to the custom archetype you've built. When you want to add new content sections to your site, you'll follow this same pattern.

Sometimes content comes from other sources, or you want other sites to be able to consume your content. Hugo has some features that let you do both, and you'll explore those next.

CHAPTER 4

Working with Data

Modern sites are driven by data. That data might come in the form of content stored in Markdown files, or from external APIs.

You've already used some data in your site. For example, you've included the site's title in your templates, and you've displayed each page's title. But you're not restricted to global configuration data. Hugo has built-in support for incorporating external data files into your site, and it can fetch data from remote sources to generate content in your layouts.

Using Site Configuration Data in Your Theme

Your layouts use {{ .Site.Title }} to display the name of the site in the browser title bar and in your header navigation. You can place all kinds of other data in your site's configuration file and use it as well.

For example, let's use the site's configuration to build additional <meta> tags in the site's header. The site configuration file has built-in fields like Title, but you can add anything you'd like to this file if you add it to a params section of the file.

Open config.toml and add a new params section that defines the author of the site and a description of the site:

```
working_with_data/portfolio/config.toml
[params]
  author = "Brian Hogan"
  description = "My portfolio site"
```

Then, open the file themes/basic/layouts/partials/head.html and add a new author meta tag to the page:

```
working_with_data/portfolio/themes/basic/layouts/partials/head.html
➤ <meta name="author" content="{{ .Site.Params.author }}">
  <link rel="stylesheet" href="{{ "css/style.css" | relURL }}">
```

Below that, add one for the description:

```
<meta name="description" content="{{ .Site.Params.description }}">
```

Now all of your pages will have these tags filled in. If you open your page in a browser and look at its source, you'll see the data:

```
    ...
    <title>Brian&#39;s Portfolio</title>
➤   <meta name="author" content="Brian Hogan">
➤   <meta name="description" content="My portfolio site">
    <link rel="stylesheet" href="/css/style.css">
    ...
```

The description field isn't page-specific yet, but you'll fix that shortly after you explore how to use front matter data to pull in content.

Adding Google Analytics

While we're on the subject of data, you might want to collect data about how people are interacting with your site. Hugo has built-in support for working with Google Analytics,[a] a platform from Google that lets you track unique page views, browser data, and other metrics from your site's visitors.

To incorporate this into your site, grab your Google Analytics tracking ID and add it to your site's configuration file using the googleAnalytics field:

```
        title = "Brian's Portfolio"
➤       googleAnalytics = "UA-xxxxxxxxxxx"
```

Then, in your themes/basic/layouts/partials/head.html file, use Hugo's built-in template:

```
{{ template "_internal/google_analytics_async.html" . }}
```

When you generate your site, the appropriate JavaScript will be added to your pages, and it'll pull the tracking ID out of your site's configuration.

If you are going to use Google Analytics or other tracking software, be sure to consult local privacy laws, as you may need to obtain permission from your users to collect data.[b]

---

a.   https://analytics.google.com/
b.   https://www.cookiepro.com/knowledge/google-analytics-and-gdpr/

Populating Page Content Using Data in Front Matter

When you created your Project archetype, you created some placeholder content that you could replace. Over time, you might want to change the content on these pages, and going through each one manually to get them all looking the same could be a lot of work.

Let's refactor the project pages so they're more data-driven.

Modify the default archetype for Projects to include the image, the image's alternative text, and the "Tech Used" content. You'll also add a summary that you can use in various places:

```
working_with_data/portfolio/archetypes/projects.md
---
title: "{{ replace .Name "-" " " | title }}"
draft: false
image: //via.placeholder.com/640x150
alt_text: "{{ replace .Name "-" " " | title }} screenshot"
summary: "Summary of the {{ replace .Name "-" " " | title }} project"
tech_used:
- JavaScript
- CSS
- HTML
---

Description of the {{ replace .Name "-" " " | title }} project...
```

Notice that you're using the name of the file to generate some of the default text for the summary, the image alt text, and even the main content.

Generate a third project using this template. Stop your server and execute the following command to create a page for a project called "Linkitivity."

```
$ hugo new projects/linkitivity.md
/Users/brianhogan/portfolio/content/projects/linkitivity.md created
```

Open content/projects/linkitivity.md and you'll see this content:

```
working_with_data/portfolio/content/projects/linkitivity.md
---
title: "Linkitivity"
draft: false
image: //via.placeholder.com/640x150
alt_text: "Linkitivity screenshot"
summary: "Summary of the Linkitivity project"
tech_used:
- JavaScript
- CSS
- HTML
---

Description of Linkitivity project...
```

The name "Linkitivity" is placed throughout the front matter, making it easier for you to maintain consistency.

Before moving on, modify the two existing project pages you created to reflect these changes. Remove the placeholder text and move it all to the front matter section instead, under those keys. For reference, here's what your Awesomeco project should look like:

```
working_with_data/portfolio/content/projects/awesomeco.md
---
title: "Awesomeco"
draft: false
image: //via.placeholder.com/640x150
alt_text: "Awesomeco screenshot"
summary: "Summary of the AwesomeCo project"
tech_used:
- JavaScript
- CSS
- HTML
---

Description of the Awesomeco project...
```

Next, modify the project layout to use this data. Open themes/basic/layouts/projects/single.html and locate the {{ .Content }} section. Below that line, add code that adds the image and alternative text from the front matter, and then iterates through the values in the tech used field to display those values on the page:

```
working_with_data/portfolio/themes/basic/layouts/projects/single.html
<section class="project">
  <h2>{{ .Title }}</h2>

  {{ .Content }}
➤ <img alt="{{ .Params.alt_text }}" src="{{ .Params.image }}">
➤
➤ <h3>Tech used</h3>
➤ <ul>
➤   {{ range .Params.tech_used }}
➤     <li>{{ . }}</li>
➤   {{ end }}
➤ </ul>

</section>
```

Notice that the image, alt_text, and tech_used fields are prefixed by .Params. Any custom fields you add to the front matter get added to this .Params collection. If you don't add that prefix, Hugo won't be able to find the data. Fields like description and title are predefined fields that Hugo knows about, so you don't need the params prefix when referencing them. You can find the list of predefined fields in Hugo's documentation.[1]

---

1. https://gohugo.io/content-management/front-matter/#predefined

Save the layout and start the development server with hugo server. Visit http://local-host:1313/projects/awesomeco.md and your project displays, but this time it's driven by front matter data instead of hard-coded content:

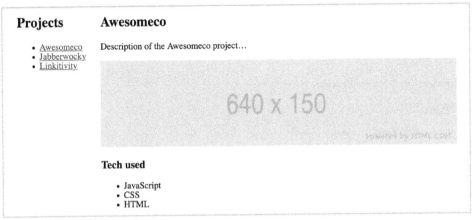

This will give you a much more uniform approach for adding projects. There's absolutely nothing wrong with continuing to define your content using the method you used before, where you used placeholder content, but you might find this method more appropriate for things that need to be developed in a more uniform fashion. However, by taking advantage of Hugo's data-driven features, it's easier to make list pages more interesting.

The information you've added to the front matter is available in other templates. Let's add the information in each project's summary field beneath each entry on the project listing page, so it's more than just a list of projects. Open themes/basic/layouts/projects/list.html and add the summary beneath the project link:

```
working_with_data/portfolio/themes/basic/layouts/projects/list.html
    {{ range .Pages }}
    <section class="project">
      <h3><a href="{{ .RelPermalink }}">{{ .Title }}</a></h3>
      <p>{{ .Summary }}</p>
    </section>
    {{ end }}
  </section>

{{ end }}
```

Save the page and visit http://localhost:1313/projects. The summaries now appear after each header as shown in the screenshot on page 40.

Remember, when you're working with range, it's iterating over each entry. Inside the block, the range is pointing at the current entry, so you can access any of the properties of that item, including content or front matter data.

Projects

This is a list of my projects. You can select each project to learn more about each one.

<u>Awesomeco</u>

Summary of the Awesomeco project

<u>Jabberwocky</u>

Summary of the Jabberwocky project

<u>Linkitivity</u>

Summary of the Linkitivity project

In addition to displaying data, you can also use the data in pages to make decisions about what to display.

Conditionally Displaying Data

Earlier in this chapter, you added a <meta> tag for the description of the page, but it's good practice to have that description reflect what's actually on the page. You can add conditional logic to your layouts to control how you display data. For example, you can check to see if there's a description field set on the page, and if there isn't, you can fall back to the site-level description.

Hugo has an isset function which, at first glance, looks like a great way to check whether a variable has a value. Unfortunately, it has limitations that aren't intuitive. It doesn't handle situations where values are always defined but are empty, like default values. The Description field on a page is actually a default field. If you don't define it in your page, its value will be defined, but empty, and isset won't work.

To handle cases where you're checking for a value in a default variable like this, use Hugo's with function. Replace the existing meta description in themes/basic/layouts/partials/head.html with this block of code, which conditionally sets the description:

```
working_with_data/portfolio/themes/basic/layouts/partials/head.html
<meta name="description" content="
  {{- with .Page.Description -}}
    {{ . }}
  {{- else -}}
    {{ .Site.Params.description }}
  {{- end -}}">
```

The with function rebinds the context. Using with, you can switch the current context to .Page.Description. Then within that block, a single period prints out the value. But the with function has a nice side effect: if the value of the context is empty, then the block gets skipped and nothing gets rendered. To handle the case where there's no description, you pair the with function with an else statement.

Save the head partial. To test this new behavior, open the content file for the project list page at content/projects/_index.md and add a description field:

working_with_data/portfolio/content/projects/_index.md
```
---
title: "Projects"
draft: false
description: A list of Brian's projects.
```

Save the changes and visit the projects list page at http://localhost:1313/projects. Inspect the source and you'll see that the description meta tag now shows the more specific description. You can now add the description field to other content pages' front matter.

> **Joe asks:**
> # What's the Difference Between summary and description in Front Matter?
>
> The difference is mostly up to you. In some cases, they might be the same content. However, the description field is great for providing a description of the page optimized for search engines or social sharing, while the summary field gives you a chance to create a short summary of the content you'll display on other parts of the site. As you'll see later in this chapter, Hugo can automatically generate a page's summary, but the summary field in the front matter overrides that, giving you more control.

The <title> element currently uses the title of the site and doesn't accurately reflect the title of an individual page. This can be bad for search engine ranking, but it's also bad from a usability standpoint. The value of the <title> tag is what appears in the browser title or bookmark tab, as well as a bookmark someone creates.

Let's use the default site title on the home page, and use the more specific page title everywhere else. To do this, use an if statement with the built-in .Site.IsHome variable to check to see if you're on the home page or not and display the site title or the more specific page title. Modify the head partial and replace the existing <title> tag with this code:

```
working_with_data/portfolio/themes/basic/layouts/partials/head.html
<title>
{{- if .Page.IsHome -}}
  {{ .Site.Title }}
{{- else -}}
  {{ .Title }} – {{ .Site.Title }}
{{- end -}}
</title>
```

Notice that this code appends the site title to the page title, which is a common practice when optimizing your site for search engines, as the page title shows up as the title in search results. With these changes in place, your page's data more accurately reflects the specific page.

Sometimes you might want to drive sections of your site from other data sources. Let's look at how to do that.

Using Local Data Files

The data directory can hold structured data files in YAML, JSON, or TOML formats that you can use in your layouts to display content. You could write these data files by hand or extract them from other sources.

Let's try this feature out and use it to add social media profile information to the contact page of the site. Instead of embedding your social media accounts in your layout directly, you'll define them in a JSON file. Then in your layout, you'll load the file and iterate over its contents and display the data.

Create the file socialmedia.json in the data directory of your site. In the new file, create an accounts property with an array of accounts. In the array, represent each account as an object with a name and url property, like this:

```
working_with_data/portfolio/data/socialmedia.json
{ "accounts" :
  [
    {
      "name": "Twitter",
      "url": "https://twitter.com/bphogan"
    },
    {
      "name": "LinkedIn",
      "url": "https://linkedin.com/in/bphogan"
    }
  ]
}
```

Save the file once you've entered in your accounts.

To use this data file, you must use a layout to read the file in and use it. Content pages can't directly include dynamic content. In Using a Shortcode to Process Images, on page 99, you'll learn how to make functions you can include in your content pages that can get dynamic content. For this example, you'll make a specific layout for the contact page of the site, instead of relying on the default single.html layout.

Add this new layout to the site's layouts directory, rather than as part of the theme, since this is a specific customization. You can incorporate this into the theme later if you find it useful. Create the file layouts/_default/contact.html and add the following boilerplate to define the main block and display the title and content:

```
working_with_data/portfolio/layouts/_default/contact.html
{{ define "main" }}
  <h2>{{ .Title }}</h2>

  {{ .Content }}

{{ end }}
```

Then, right below the {{ .Content }} line, add this code, which loads the data and iterates over it:

```
working_with_data/portfolio/layouts/_default/contact.html
<h3>Social Media</h3>
<ul>
  {{ range .Site.Data.socialmedia.accounts }}
    <li><a href="{{ .url }}">{{ .name }}</a></li>
  {{ end }}
</ul>
```

Save the file. The layout you created won't override the default single page layout because it's not associated with a specific type of content. When you created a layout for projects, Hugo automatically associated the layout with all content within the projects folder. In this case, there's no association like that, so you have to explicitly assign the layout file to the contact.md Markdown file. Open content/contact.md and specify the contact layout in the page's front matter by adding the following code:

```
working_with_data/portfolio/content/contact.md
---
title: "Contact"
date: 2020-01-01T12:55:44-05:00
draft: false
➤ layout: contact
---

This is my Contact page.
```

Save the file, fire up the development server with `hugo server`, visit http://local-host:1313/contact in your browser. Your social media links are now displayed on the page:

Contact

Social Media

- Twitter
- LinkedIn

Sometimes the data you want comes from an external site. Let's look at how to handle that.

Pulling Data from Remote Sources

You're not limited to using local data. You can use Hugo to fetch remote data and process it every time you build the site.

Let's create a page of the site that shows your public GitHub repositories.

To get that data, you will use the GitHub API and then make a request to https://api.github.com/users/<your username>/repos. This returns a JSON collection of all your repositories and doesn't require any authorization.

Store the API URL and your GitHub username in the site's configuration file, rather than directly in the layout. Open config.toml and add two new fields to the params section to hold these values:

```
working_with_data/portfolio/config.toml
[params]
  author = "Brian Hogan"
  description = "My portfolio site"

➤ gh_url = "https://api.github.com/users"
➤ gh_user = "your-gh-user"
```

Then, create a layout for this file in themes/basic/layouts/_default/opensource.html. Unlike the contact page you created, you'll keep this with your theme. Add the usual boilerplate to the file:

```
working_with_data/portfolio/themes/basic/layouts/_default/opensource.html
{{ define "main" }}
  <h2>{{ .Title }}</h2>

  {{ .Content }}
{{ end }}
```

Next, right after the {{ .Content }} line, add the following line of code to build up the GitHub URL using your username from the site's configuration:

```
working_with_data/portfolio/themes/basic/layouts/_default/opensource.html
{{ $url := printf "%s/%s/repos" .Site.Params.gh_url .Site.Params.gh_user }}
```

This defines a $url variable and uses Go's printf function to concatenate the base URL, your username, and the /repos endpoint. Note that you have to use .Site.Params as a prefix on both of these, as you stored them in the site's configuration.

Now, add this line to make the request for the JSON file using the $url variable you built:

```
working_with_data/portfolio/themes/basic/layouts/_default/opensource.html
{{ $repos := getJSON $url }}
```

This makes the request and fetches the JSON data into a collection that works like the other collections you've used. From here, you can use the range function and iterate over the results. Each result has a name, url, html_url, and description property, so use those to build a list of your repositories, like this:

```
working_with_data/portfolio/themes/basic/layouts/_default/opensource.html
<section class="oss">
  {{ range $repos }}
    <article>
      <h3><a href="{{ .html_url }}">{{ .name }}</a></h3>
      <p>{{ .description }}</p>
    </article>
  {{ end }}
</section>
```

The html_url property points to the URL of the repository, while the url property points to the API endpoint, which you could use if you wanted to fetch even more details about each project.

Every time you rebuild the site, Hugo will make a request to the GitHub API and pull in this data. Since the data about your repositories doesn't change that often, this level of caching is perfect. However, if you don't want to hit the API every time you build, you can download the JSON data, store it in your data directory, and load it in like you did with your social media links on the contact. If you take this approach, remember to refresh your local file periodically.

Next, create a new content page for your site called opensource.md which will use this layout. Stop the development server and use the hugo new command to create this file:

```
$ hugo new opensource.md
```

Open the newly created content/opensource.md file in your editor. Ensure the draft status is false, set the title to "Open Source Software", and ensure it uses the opensource layout. Below the front matter, add a paragraph of content that introduces the page content. Your completed file should look like this:

working_with_data/portfolio/content/opensource.md
```
---
title: "Open Source Software"
date: 2020-01-01T13:35:47-05:00
draft: false
layout: opensource
---

My Open Source Software on GitHub:
```

Let's add some CSS to transform the list into a series of tiles. Open themes/basic/static/css/style.css and add the following code:

working_with_data/portfolio/themes/basic/static/css/style.css
```
.oss {
  display: flex;
  flex-wrap: wrap;
  justify-content: space-between;
}

.oss article {
  border: 1px solid #ddd;
  box-shadow: 3px 3px 3px #ddd;
  margin: 0.5%;
  padding: 0.5%;
  width: 30%;
}
```

Flexbox once again comes to the rescue. The oss container becomes the flex container and specifies that child elements should wrap and be spaced out equally. The inner article elements get a width, margin, a border and a small drop shadow. The result is a series of tiles nicely spaced apart.

Ensure all of your files are saved and start up the development server with hugo server. Visit http://localhost:1313/opensource and you'll see your projects displayed as tiles as shown in the screenshot on page 47.

Now, whenever you create a new project on GitHub, it'll show up when you regenerate the site.

Open Source Software

My Open Source Software on GitHub:

Lorem	Ipsum	Dolor
Lorem ipsum dolor sit amet, consectetur adipisicing elit.	Lorem ipsum dolor sit amet, consectetur adipisicing elit.	Lorem ipsum dolor sit amet, consectetur adipisicing elit.

Joe asks:

How Would I Generate Content Pages from Data?

Hugo is a static site generator that converts existing content documents into web pages. It doesn't have any built-in ability to generate content pages from data, but you can still make it work.

For example, you could write a small script that reads the data and generates Markdown documents, which it stores in the content folder. Then, when you run hugo to build the site, the generated pages will be included.

Hugo's developers want Hugo to stay focused on fast website generation. As a result, you'll often find that you'll rely on tools outside of Hugo for more complex situations.

Before moving on, add the link to your open source projects page to your project list page. Open themes/basic/layouts/projects/list.html and add the link on the page like this, along with its summary:

working_with_data/portfolio/themes/basic/layouts/projects/list.html
```
<section class="projects">
➤   <section class="project">
➤   {{ with .Site.GetPage "/opensource.md" }}
➤     <h3><a href="{{ .RelPermalink }}">{{ .Title }}</a></h3>
➤     <p>{{ .Summary }}</p>
➤   {{ end }}
➤   </section>
```

Instead of using a hard-coded link, you're grabbing the title and URL from the page using Hugo's GetPage function, which takes the path to the Markdown file. Using this method, you can pull data from any page into your layouts.

The front matter for the open source page doesn't have a summary field, so you're probably wondering where the summary will come from. Hugo gets it by reading in the first few sentences of the content for that page. You'll take more control of auto-generated summaries in Chapter 5, Adding a Blog, on page 55.

Visit http://localhost:1313/projects to see your open source projects displayed above the other projects:

> ## Projects
>
> This is a list of my projects. You can select each project to learn more about each one.
>
> ### Open Source Software
>
> My Open Source Software on GitHub:
>
> ### Awesomeco
>
> Summary of the Awesomeco project

So far you've used Hugo to generate HTML pages, but you can also generate other formats too.

Syndicating Content with RSS

Hugo creates RSS feeds for your site automatically using a built-in RSS 2.0 template. If you visit http://localhost:1313/index.xml, you'll find a pre-built RSS feed that includes all of your pages and looks something like this:

```
<?xml version="1.0" encoding="utf-8" standalone="yes" ?>
<rss version="2.0" xmlns:atom="http://www.w3.org/2005/Atom">
  <channel>
    <title>Brian&#39;s Portfolio</title>
    <link>http://localhost:1313/</link>
    <description>Recent content on Brian&#39;s Portfolio</description>
    <generator>Hugo -- gohugo.io</generator>
    <language>en-us</language>
    <lastBuildDate>Thu, 02 Jan 2020 12:45:51 -0600</lastBuildDate>

    <atom:link href="http://localhost:1313/index.xml" rel="self"
        type="application/rss+xml" />

    <item>
      <title>Open Source Software</title>
      <link>http://localhost:1313/opensource/</link>
      <pubDate>Thu, 02 Jan 2020 12:42:17 -0500</pubDate>

      <guid>http://localhost:1313/opensource/</guid>
      <description>My Open Source Software:</description>
    </item>
...

  </channel>
</rss>
```

Hugo generates RSS feeds for your sections too. Your projects have their own feed at http://localhost:1313/projects/index.xml.

People won't know there's a feed for your site unless you tell them about it. To make your feed discoverable, you can add a meta tag to your site's header that looks like this:

```
<link rel="alternate" type="application/rss+xml"
href="http://example.com/feed" >
```

RSS readers and other tools can use this tag to identify the RSS feed automatically.

Add this code to your themes/basic/layouts/partials/head.html file to add links to any alternative formats associated with your page:

```
working_with_data/portfolio/themes/basic/layouts/partials/head.html
{{ range .AlternativeOutputFormats -}}
  {{- $link := `<link rel="%s" type="%s" href="%s" title="%s">` -}}
  {{- $title := printf "%s - %s" $.Page.Title $.Site.Title -}}

  {{- if $.Page.IsHome -}}
    {{ $title = $.Site.Title }}
  {{- end -}}

  {{ printf $link .Rel .MediaType.Type .Permalink $title | safeHTML }}
{{- end }}
```

This iterates over all of the alternative formats associated with the current page. Right now there's only one, but you may add more in the future. Each content has a type attribute. Hugo will attempt to escape special characters when you print values using the {{ }} notation. One of those values is the plus sign in application/rss+xml, the value associated with RSS feeds.

To avoid escaping special characters, use the printf function to inject the values. Note the backticks around the value for the $link variable. By using the backticks, you don't need to escape the double-quotes for the HTML attributes.

The title attribute should reflect the title of the page, so you detect if this is the home page or not, and assign the proper title to the $title variable. This is similar to how you set the value for the <title> tag. However, since the range function is operating on the collection of alternative formats, the current scope is limited to values in that collection. Prefixing the scope with a dollar sign tells Hugo that you're looking for values in the global scope rather than in the current local scope. That is why you use $.Page.isHome here instead of .Page.isHome.

The final printf statement creates the <link> tag. The safeHTML at the end ensures the HTML snippet itself isn't escaped. Be careful with safeHTML; only use it with HTML snippets you create, and use it sparingly. Never use it on snippets you don't trust.

When you visit http://localhost:1313/ in your browser and look at its source, you'll see the RSS link generated:

```
<link rel="alternate" type="application/rss+xml"
href="http://localhost:1313/index.xml" title="Brian's Portfolio">
```

Since this link to the feed is generated using the .Permalink function, Hugo will use the value of the baseURL field in the config.toml file when you build the site. When it comes time to deploy the site, you'll specify that value so everything works properly.

If you visit http://localhost:1313/projects/, you'll see the link for that page as well:

```
<link rel="alternate" type="application/rss+xml"
href="http://localhost:1313/projects/index.xml"
title="Projects - Brian's Portfolio">
```

Hugo can support many output formats. Let's use Hugo to generate a JSON file that lists your projects.

Rendering Content as JSON

Hugo supports JSON output out of the box too, which means you can use Hugo to create a JSON API that you can consume from other applications. Unlike RSS feeds, you need to create a layout for your JSON output, and you must specify which pages of your site should use this output type.

To explore this, you'll make a JSON list of your project pages containing the title and URL for each project page, which you can then consume from other applications. The resulting file will look like this:

```
{
  "projects": [
    {
      "url": "http://example.org/projects/awesomeco/",
      "title": "Awesomeco",
    },
    {
      "url": "http://example.org/projects/jabberwocky/",
      "title": "Jabberwocky",
    }
  ]
}
```

First, create a JSON template file at themes/basic/layouts/projects/list.json.

In the new template file, create a JSON template that iterates through your project pages and displays them:

```
working_with_data/portfolio/themes/basic/layouts/projects/list.json
{
  "projects": [
    {{- range $index, $page := (where .Site.RegularPages "Type" "in" "projects") }}
    {{- if $index -}} , {{- end }}
    {
      "url": {{ .Permalink | jsonify }},
      "title": {{ .Title | jsonify }}
    }
    {{- end }}
  ]
}
```

Entries in a JSON array need a comma between each entry, but they don't need a comma after the last entry. By using an index as you iterate through the entries, you can insert the comma in front of the current entry. Note that you're using the {{- form for the templates, which suppresses whitespace in the output, depending on where the dash is located. Remember from Using Content Blocks and Partials, on page 17, that adding the dash after the opening braces suppresses whitespace characters in front of the output, while adding a dash in front of the closing braces suppresses whitespace that follows. Suppressing whitespace like this will result in JSON that's more readable by humans.

Hugo won't generate the JSON file until you configure it to do so. You can configure output formats in the main configuration file, but you can only specify that for the home page, all sections, and all content pages. To apply the output to a specific section of the site, you specify it in the front matter of the section's page.

In this case, the output formats need to be specified in the project list content page. Edit the file content/projects/_index.md and add the following front matter to tell Hugo to generate a JSON file in addition to the HTML and XML files it generates by default:

```
working_with_data/portfolio/content/projects/_index.md
description: A list of Brian's projects.
➤ outputs:
➤ - HTML
➤ - JSON
➤ - RSS
```

Save the file and then run hugo server. Visit http://localhost:1313/projects/index.json and you'll see your file.

You might be thinking that the URL is a little ugly, and you'd like to change it to /projects.json instead. The url field in a page's front matter lets you change the URL for a page, like this:

```
url: /projects.json
```

Unfortunately, if you add that line to the content/projects/_index.md file, Hugo will no longer render the HTML page. Hugo doesn't have a way to handle different URLs for different types. If you wanted to change the URL for your project feed, you have two options.

The first option is to configure your web server to rewrite the URL. The second (and much easier) option is to move the file before you upload it to your server. In other words, move projects/index.json to projects.json. You could do this as part of a larger build and deploy process like the one you'll create in Using Webpack and npm with Hugo, on page 102.

One last thing: if you visit http://localhost:1313/projects/ and look at its source, you'll see a <link> tag for your JSON feed next to your RSS feed. The loop you created to display your RSS feed iterates through all of the alternative formats for a page, so this JSON feed gets included.

Your Turn

Before moving on, see if you can complete these challenges:

1. Add keywords to the front matter of your home page and content pages, and add a <meta name="keywords"> tag to your site's heading.

2. Change the footer so it uses the author name in the site's configuration file in the copyright notice.

3. Incorporate the social media links into your site's footer. Include the code in a partial.

4. Download your repository data to a local JSON file and modify the template to read that local file instead. Once you have it working, revert the change so the data is pulled directly from GitHub again.

5. Dive deeper into how whitespace suppression works in Hugo templates by adding and removing dashes in your list.json template. Make a change and

then review the source of the file in the browser. Notice how changing {{ to {{- or }} to -}} affects how the JSON is formatted.

6. Add additional fields to the JSON file for your project feed.

Wrapping Up

You've integrated some JSON data into your site. You've got social media links coming from a local file, and you've loaded your GitHub repositories from GitHub's public-facing API. In addition, you used data from the configuration file and individual front matter sections throughout your site. Combined with what you've learned in previous chapters, you have all the tools to add a blog to your personal site, which you'll do next.

CHAPTER 5

Adding a Blog

When you want to share your thoughts with the world, using your own site is one of the best ways to do it. While there are platforms you can use to do this, choosing to instead host from your own domain offers certain benefits. You can measure its effects, control how the information is presented, and more importantly, build your own brand with content you own. When you publish content elsewhere, you have to opt in to their terms of service, and sometimes hand over control over your content and community.

To simplify the process of hosting your own content, you can use Hugo to add a blog to your site. To create a blog in Hugo, you'll create a new content type, named "Post", and you'll create layouts to support displaying those posts. A lot of what you'll do in this chapter will build on what you've done previously, but you'll apply it in new ways. In addition to creating the content type, you'll incorporate a third-party commenting system into your static site, and you'll implement pagination so you can support future content growth.

A post on a blog has a title, an author, and some content. It might have a summary as well. You might want to put your posts into categories and tag them. You can manage most of this from the front matter of each piece of content much like you did with projects.

Start by creating an archetype for a post so you have a blueprint to follow. Create the file archetypes/posts.md by copying the default archetype file:

blog/portfolio/archetypes/posts.md
```
---
title: "{{ replace .Name "-" " " | title }}"
date: {{ .Date }}
draft: false
---
```

Then, add an author field and add your name:

```
blog/portfolio/archetypes/posts.md
author: Brian Hogan
```

Next, add some default content to this file. Any placeholder text will do, like Lorem Ipsum:[1]

```
blog/portfolio/archetypes/posts.md
Lorem ipsum dolor sit amet, consectetur adipisicing elit, sed do eiusmod
tempor incididunt ut labore et dolore magna aliqua.

<!--more-->

Ut enim ad minim veniam, quis nostrud exercitation ullamco laboris nisi ut
aliquip ex ea commodo consequat.
```

The <!--more--> line lets you specify where the content summary ends. As you learned in Pulling Data from Remote Sources, on page 44, when you use {{ .Summary }} in a layout, Hugo will pull the summary from the front matter or by generating it from the content. Sometimes that auto-generated summary ends in an awkward place. To control where the summary should end, add <!--more--> to the content.

Save the archetype and use it to generate an initial post to test things out:

```
$ hugo new posts/first-post.md
/Users/brianhogan/portfolio/content/posts/first-post.md created
```

Visit http://localhost:1313/posts/ and you'll see your post listed. This list is generated using the default list layout, which you'll customize later. Let's flesh out the layout for an individual post.

Creating the Post's Layout

The page for an individual post is bare because it's using the default single page layout. Like with project pages, there's information in each post's front matter you can use on the page. To do that, create a new single page layout for posts.

Create the directory themes/basic/layouts/posts/ to hold the layout. You can use your editor or use the following command in your terminal:

```
$ mkdir themes/basic/layouts/posts
```

Then create the file themes/basic/layouts/posts/single.html, which will hold the layout for an individual post.

Create the main content block and place the title and post content in their own sectioning elements with classes; this will help you style them later:

---

1.   https://www.lipsum.com/

```
blog/portfolio/themes/basic/layouts/posts/single.html
{{ define "main" }}
<article class="post">
  <header>
    <h2>{{ .Title }}</h2>
  </header>

  <section class="body">
    {{ .Content }}
  </section>

</article>
{{ end }}
```

Within the `header` section, add the byline, which will contain the publication date and author name. The .Date field will fetch the date, and the .Format function will let you format it in a similar fashion to how you formatted the date in the footer.

```
blog/portfolio/themes/basic/layouts/posts/single.html
  <header>
    <h2>{{ .Title }}</h2>
➤   <p>
➤     By {{ .Params.Author }}
➤   </p>
➤   <p>
➤     Posted {{ .Date.Format "January 2, 2006" }}
➤   </p>
```

Many blogs will display the amount of time it takes to read the content at the top of an article. Let's add that to our blog page template.

The average person reads anywhere from 200 to 250 words per minute[2] depending on several factors. If you count the number of words in a page's content and divide it by 200, you'll get a conservative estimate of the number of minutes it'll take to read your content.

Hugo has built-in functions for counting words and doing math, so in your template, add the following code to your byline to determine and display the reading time:

```
blog/portfolio/themes/basic/layouts/posts/single.html
    <p>
      Posted {{ .Date.Format "January 2, 2006" }}
    </p>
➤   <p>
➤     Reading time: {{ math.Round (div (countwords .Content) 200.0) }} minutes.
➤   </p>
```

---

2. https://www.irisreading.com/what-is-the-average-reading-speed/

To make sure this works, add a significant amount of content to your first blog post so there's some text to count.

Save the file and visit http://localhost:1313/posts/first-post.md. The author, date, and reading time display above the post:

First Post

By Brian Hogan

Posted January 1, 2020

Reading time: 2 minutes.

Lorem ipsum dolor sit amet, consectetur adipisicing elit, sed do eiusmod tempor incididunt ut labore et dolore magna aliqua.

Ut enim ad minim veniam, quis nostrud exercitation ullamco laboris nisi ut aliquip ex ea commodo consequat.

As you build out more content, you'll probably want to organize and group it so it's easier for people to find.

Organizing Content with Taxonomies

Many blogs and content systems let you place your posts in categories and apply tags to your posts. This logical grouping of content is known as a *taxonomy*. Hugo supports categories and tags out of the box and can generate category and tag list pages automatically. All you have to do is add categories and tags to your front matter.

Open the posts archetype at archetypes/post.md and add some default categories and tags:

```
blog/portfolio/archetypes/posts.md
categories:
- Personal
- Thoughts
tags:
- software
- html
```

Adding these defaults to the archetype won't affect the content you've already created, so open content/posts/first-post.md and add categories and tags there too:

```
blog/portfolio/content/posts/first-post.md
categories:
- Personal
- Thoughts
tags:
- software
- html
```

> **Joe asks:**
> # Does Hugo Support Syntax Highlighting for Code?
>
> If you're publishing posts, you might want to include snippets of code from time to time. Hugo supports syntax highlighting using a library named Chroma,[a] which is compatible with the popular Pygments[b] syntax highlighter.
>
> To configure this, tell Hugo you want it to use Pygments-style classes when it highlights your code. Add this line to config.toml:
>
> ```
> pygmentsUseClasses = true
> ```
>
> Then, generate a stylesheet to highlight your code using one of the available Chroma styles:[c]
>
> ```
> $ hugo gen chromastyles --style=github &gt; syntax.css
> ```
>
> Add the syntax.css style to your head.html partial.
>
> Now, when you write your posts, use code fences and specify the appropriate language:
>
> ```
> ```javascript
> let x = 25;
> let y = 30;
> ```
> ```
>
> Hugo will apply the styles to your code.
>
> _____
> a.    https://github.com/alecthomas/chroma
> b.    https://pygments.org/
> c.    https://xyproto.github.io/splash/docs/

Both categories and tags are lists of items, so you need to use the correct notation in YAML. Hugo supports TOML and JSON front matter as well, so you could use those for your posts instead if you find those easier to manage.

By adding the tags and categories to your post, Hugo will generate pages for those using your default list layout. Visit http://localhost:1313/tags to see the tags list:

Tags

- html
- software

Selecting a tag shows you a list of all of the pieces of content associated with that tag.

Visit https://localhost:1313/categories to see the list of categories:

Categories

- [Personal](#)
- [Thoughts](#)

When you visit https://localhost:1313/tags, you're looking at what Hugo calls "taxonomy terms." When you look at a specific tag, that's what Hugo calls a "taxonomy." This becomes important when you'd like to customize the layouts for these pages. Let's alter the tags list so it shows the count of items associated with each tag in addition to the tag.

To customize the page that displays the list of all of your tags, create a new layout named tag.terms.html. Place it in themes/basic/layouts/_default/.

In the new file, add the usual layout boilerplate, including the title and the {{ .Content }} pieces. Instead of iterating over the related pages like you have done in previous list templates, iterate over all of the tags for the site with .Data.Terms. This will give you access to the number of content pages associated with each tag:

```
blog/portfolio/themes/basic/layouts/_default/tag.terms.html
{{ define "main" }}

  <h2>{{ .Title }}</h2>

  {{ .Content }}

  {{ range .Data.Terms.Alphabetical }}
  <p class="tag">
    <a href="{{ .Page.Permalink }}">{{ .Page.Title }}</a>
    <span class="count">({{ .Count }})</span>
  </p>
  {{ end }}

{{ end }}
```

You've included {{ .Content }} in the layout. When you're looking at the /tags section of the site, Hugo will look in content/tags/_index.md for that content. Create the _index.md file now using:

```
$ hugo new tags/_index.md
/Users/brianhogan/portfolio/content/tags/_index.md created
```

Open the file in your editor and add some content:

```
blog/portfolio/content/tags/_index.md
---
title: "Tags"
date: 2020-01-01T15:17:39-05:00
draft: false
---

These are the site's tags:
```

Now, visit http://localhost:1313/tags and you'll see your tag list with counts and the associated content:

Tags

These are the site's tags:

html (1)

software (1)

When you select a tag, Hugo looks for a layout associated with tags. If you want to customize this layout, create a layout named tags.html in the theme/basic/layouts/_default folder and use the same logic you use in your existing list layout to pull in the content. When you're displaying content for a specific tag, you're not interested in the collection of tags; you're interested in the pages associated with the tag.

Before moving on, add the list of tags to the post's single layout. Open themes/basic/layouts/posts/single.html.

To display the tags, iterate over the tags in the front matter using .Params.tags and the range function:

```
blog/portfolio/themes/basic/layouts/posts/single.html
    <p>
      By {{ .Params.Author }}
    </p>
    <p>
      Posted {{ .Date.Format "January 2, 2006" }}
➤     <span class="tags">
➤       in
➤       {{ range .Params.tags }}
➤         <a class="tag" href="/tags/{{ . | urlize }}">{{ . }}</a>
➤       {{ end }}
➤     </span>
    </p>
```

The tags listing page is located at /tags, and each tag itself is located at /tags/tag-name. As you iterate over each tag, you can construct the link to each tag by appending the tag name to /tags/. However, since tags might contain spaces or other characters, use the urlize function to encode the tag as a URL-safe string.

Each link in the tag list has a class of tag so you can more easily style the entries in the list. Open themes/basic/static/css/style.css and add the following CSS to change each tag into a gray button:

blog/portfolio/themes/basic/static/css/style.css
```
a.tag {
  background-color: #ddd;
  color: #333;
  display: inline-block;
  padding: 0.1em;
  font-size: 0.9em;
  text-decoration: none;
}
```

When you add padding to each tag so that the background color doesn't touch the words, the boxes will become larger, so you can decrease the font size to make up the difference.

Visit http://localhost:1313/posts/first-post to see the updated byline with the tag list:

First Post

By Brian Hogan

Posted January 1, 2020 in software   html

Reading time: 2 minutes.

Your individual post page looks good, and you've got tags and categories configured. Now let's look at customizing the URLs for your posts.

Customizing the URL for Posts

By default, your blog contents show up under posts/. For example, your first blog post is available at http://localhost:1313/posts/first-post. Many blogs use the year/month/title format for their blog post URLs. This meaningful URL shows anyone looking at the URL how old the post might be, but it also shows that

Disabling Taxonomies

By default, Hugo generates category and tag pages for you. But if you have no interest in tags, you can configure your site to ignore then. In your config.toml file, add the following code:

```
[taxonomies]
  category = "categories"
```

By doing this, you're redefining the taxonomies to exclude tags. If you wanted tags but not categories, you'd add this code instead:

```
[taxonomies]
  tag = "tags"
```

If you don't want Hugo to use any kind of taxonomy, you can disable it entirely by adding this option to the configuration instead:

```
disableKinds = ["taxonomy", "taxonomyTerm"]
```

This removes all support for taxonomies on your site, so take care with this option.

the content is organized by date. In sites with content organized like this, a visitor could see content for the rest of the month, or for the whole year, by specifying the year or month.

A *permalink* is a permanent link to a specific page, often used when sharing a page with others through social media, newsletters, or even search results. You can use front matter on a post to control the permalink for a post by using the url field, but that's really only meant to handle situations where you're migrating content or need to do some one-off customization. Hugo lets you define how you'd like to structure your links in its configuration file.

In config.toml, add a new Permalinks section and define a new rule that makes posts available under /posts/year/month/slug:

```
blog/portfolio/config.toml
[permalinks]
  posts = "posts/:year/:month/:slug/"
```

This gives you URLs like /posts/2020/01/first_post. The *slug* is the end part of the URL that identifies the page's content. It's generated from the page title by default, but you can define your own slug by adding a slug field to your page's front matter section.

If you visit /posts/2020, you might expect to find a list of all posts for that year. Unfortunately, Hugo doesn't support generating these pages currently, at least not without a little extra work.

However, one of Hugo's maintainers offered a practical workaround.[3] By using Hugo's taxonomy feature and a little clever use of front matter, you can generate archive pages of posts for years and months. You're going to add "year" and "month" as new taxonomies, and "tag" your posts with a year and month. Hugo can then build the year and month pages for you just like it builds pages for categories and tags. You'll use this approach with some minor tweaks to build out your pages.

First, add year and month fields to your content's front matter. For the year, use the four digit year. For the month, use the four digit year, a forward slash, and the two digit month. For example, for a post written in January of 2020, you'd add these fields:

```
year: "2020"
month: "2020/01"
```

Open content/posts/first-post.md and add the year and month fields:

```
blog/portfolio/content/posts/first-post.md
title: "First Post"
date: 2020-01-01T14:17:39-05:00
draft: false
author: Brian Hogan
➤ year: "2020"
➤ month: "2020/01"
```

Adding these fields every time you create new content on your blog is going to get old pretty quickly, and it feels redundant. You can generate these in your posts.md archetype. It's already getting the date, so create these fields in the archetype and extract the month and year:

```
blog/portfolio/archetypes/posts.md
year: "{{ dateFormat "2006" .Date }}"
month: "{{ dateFormat "2006/01" .Date }}"
```

The dateFormat function uses Hugo's date formatting strings and applies them to the given date. Now when you generate new pages for your site, the month and year front matter will be created. Create a new post for your site to verify that these front matter changes work:

```
$ hugo new posts/second-post.md
/Users/brianhogan/portfolio/content/posts/second-post.md created
```

---

3. https://discourse.gohugo.io/t/how-to-generate-chronological-blog-archives-in-hugo/13491/6

Open content/posts/second-post.md to verify that the month and year is set:

blog/portfolio/content/posts/second-post.md

```
---
title: "Second Post"
date: 2020-01-01T14:25:39-05:00
draft: false
➤ year: "2020"
➤ month: "2020/09"
author: Brian Hogan
```

Next, open your site's configuration file and define permalinks for the year and month pages. Add this code:

blog/portfolio/config.toml

```
[permalinks]
  posts = "posts/:year/:month/:slug/"
➤  year = "/posts/:slug/"
➤  month = "/posts/:slug/"
```

Finally, to generate the archive lists, define the year and month data as new taxonomies. To do this, add a taxonomies section to the configuration file, like this:

blog/portfolio/config.toml

```
[taxonomies]
  year = "year"
  month = "month"
  tag = "tags"
  category = "categories"
```

When you define a taxonomies section in your configuration, it replaces the defaults. To keep support for tags and categories, you have to explicitly define them now that you've customized things.

Save the configuration file. Your default list layout will handle the actual display of the posts, so when you visit /posts/<year> or /posts/<year>/<month>, the posts for that section will show.

They don't look very good, though, so let's fix that.

Customizing Blog List Pages

The list of posts isn't very appealing since we're using the default list layout. Let's make a layout for posts that shows the title, post date, and a summary of each post's content.

You'll need to make a main posts list showing the most recent posts, but you'll want to do the same thing for your "year" and "month" list pages. Since there's going to be significant duplication, you can make a partial to hold the bulk of the markup for a post and share that across layouts.

Start by adding that partial. Create the file themes/basic/layouts/partials/post_summary.html. In the file, add the following code, which renders the post's title, publication date, and summary in an <article> element:

```
blog/portfolio/themes/basic/layouts/partials/post_summary.html
<article>
  <header>
    <h3>
      <a href="{{ .RelPermalink }}">{{ .Title }}</a>
    </h3>
    <time>
      {{ .Date | dateFormat "January" }}
      {{ .Date | dateFormat "2" }}
    </time>
  </header>

  {{ .Summary }}

</article>
```

Save the file. Now create the file themes/basic/layouts/posts/list.html and add the following code, which iterates over the pages and uses the partial to display them:

```
blog/portfolio/themes/basic/layouts/posts/list.html
{{ define "main" }}
  <h2>{{ .Title }}</h2>

  {{ range .Pages }}
    {{ partial "post_summary.html" . }}
  {{ end }}

{{ end }}
```

Save the file and visit http://localhost:1313/posts to see it in action. Each post displays, with the most recent post first, and its abstract displays as well:

Posts

Second Post

January 1

Lorem ipsum dolor sit amet, consectetur adipisicing elit, sed do eiusmod tempor incididunt ut labore et dolore magna aliqua.

First Post

January 1

Lorem ipsum dolor sit amet, consectetur adipisicing elit, sed do eiusmod tempor incididunt ut labore et dolore magna aliqua.

This layout only works for posts. It won't work for taxonomy pages like your year and month archive pages. To make that work, you'll need more specific layouts. You defined the year and month pages as new taxonomies, so create the files year.html and month.html in the themes/basic/layouts/_default directory with the same code as the post list layout. To speed up the process, copy the existing list page. You can do that your editor, or with the following commands if you're using macOS, Linux, or WSL:

```
$ cd themes/basic/layouts
$ cp posts/list.html _default/year.html
$ cp posts/list.html _default/month.html
$ cd -
```

The cd - command returns you to the previous directory.

Once those files are in place, start up the server again with hugo server and visit http://localhost:1313/posts/2020. You'll see the posts for that year displayed:

2020

Second Post

January 1

Lorem ipsum dolor sit amet, consectetur adipisicing elit, sed do eiusmod tempor incididunt ut labore et dolore magna aliqua.

First Post

January 1

Lorem ipsum dolor sit amet, consectetur adipisicing elit, sed do eiusmod tempor incididunt ut labore et dolore magna aliqua.

With your list page complete, add your blog to the site's navigation bar. Open themes/basic/layouts/partials/nav.html and add a link to your posts page:

```
blog/portfolio/themes/basic/layouts/partials/nav.html
<nav>
  <a href="/">Home</a>
  <a href="/about">About</a>
➤ <a href="/posts">Blog</a>
  <a href="/projects">Projects</a>
  <a href="/resume">Résumé</a>
  <a href="/contact">Contact</a>
</nav>
```

Save the file. Your navigation bar now contains a link to your blog.

As you get more content, your list page might become quite long. You can break things up with pagination.

Adding Pagination

Once you have more than a handful of posts, your archives pages are going to get very long. And your main blog list page will grow and grow until it's too big to be useful. To handle this, you can break up the list of results into multiple pages, with links to navigate between the list pages. This process is known as *pagination*.

Hugo has built-in pagination support, and it's enabled by default. All you have to do is change how you fetch pages and add pagination navigation to your layouts.

To use pagination, use .Paginator.Pages instead of .Pages in your range statement, like this:

```
{{ range .Paginator.Pages }}
```

Hugo defaults to showing 10 pages at a time with its paginator, but you can override this in the layout. Let's explore this by applying pagination to the list layout for posts.

First, create another post in your site so you have more than two pages. Use hugo new to create the page:

```
$ hugo new posts/third-post.md
/Users/brianhogan/portfolio/content/posts/third-post.md created
```

Then, open themes/basic/layouts/posts/list.html and modify it to use the paginator and the built-in pagination template. For now, set the number of pages to show to 1 since you only have three pages and you'll want to be able to test out the navigation:

```
blog/portfolio/themes/basic/layouts/posts/list_with_pagination.html
{{ define "main" }}
  <h2>{{ .Title }}</h2>

➤  {{ range (.Paginator 1).Pages }}
    {{ partial "post_summary.html" . }}
  {{ end }}

➤  {{ template "_internal/pagination.html" . }}

{{ end }}
```

Save the file. When you view the site, the pagination won't look very pretty as shown in the screenshot on page 69.

Posts

Third Post

January 1

Lorem ipsum dolor sit amet, consectetur adipisicing elit, sed do eiusmod aliqua.

- ««
- «
- 1
- 2
- 3
- »
- »»

Hugo's internal pagination template uses markup compatible with Bootstrap,[4] the popular CSS framework. Since you're not using Bootstrap in this theme, you'll have to whip up a few styles. If you view the source of your page in the browser, you'll see markup like this for the pagination:

```
<ul class="pagination">
  <li class="page-item">
    <a href="/posts/" class="page-link" aria-label="First">
      <span aria-hidden="true">&laquo;&laquo;</span>
    </a>
  </li>
  <li class="page-item disabled">
    <a href="" class="page-link" aria-label="Previous">
      <span aria-hidden="true">&laquo;</span>
    </a>
  </li>
  <li class="page-item active"><a class="page-link" href="/posts/">1</a></li>
  <li class="page-item"><a class="page-link" href="/posts/page/2/">2</a></li>
  <li class="page-item"><a class="page-link" href="/posts/page/3/">3</a></li>
  <li class="page-item">
    <a href="/posts/page/2/" class="page-link" aria-label="Next">
      <span aria-hidden="true">&raquo;</span>
    </a>
  </li>
  <li class="page-item">
    <a href="/posts/page/3/" class="page-link" aria-label="Last">
      <span aria-hidden="true">&raquo;&raquo;</span>
    </a>
  </li>
</ul>
```

---

4. https://getbootstrap.com/

Hugo's pagination template generated a list of links with various classes that you can use to style the elements. There are classes to identify the active elements, disabled elements, and regular elements.

To style this quickly, use a method similar to how you styled the navbar and use Flexbox. Open the themes/basic/static/css/style.css file in your editor and add the following code to style the pagination container:

blog/portfolio/themes/basic/static/css/style.css
```
.pagination {
  display: flex;
  justify-content: space-between;
  list-style: none;
  margin: 1em auto;
  padding: 0;
}

@media only screen and (min-width: 768px) {
  .pagination {
    width: 30%;
  }
}
```

On larger screens, you constrain the width to be 30% of the page. The margin: 0 auto line centers the element horizontally.

Next, add this code to define how each pagination button looks by giving it a border and some width:

blog/portfolio/themes/basic/static/css/style.css
```
.pagination > .page-item {
  border: 1px solid #ddd;
  flex: 1;
  text-align: center;
  width: 5em;
}
```

Then style the individual links. Set each link to display: block so it fills the parent container. This makes the links easier to click, as the click target is the entire box, rather than the text:

blog/portfolio/themes/basic/static/css/style.css
```
.pagination .page-link {
  display: block;
  color: #000;
  text-decoration: none;
}
```

Finally, add code to change the colors for the active page link and the disabled links:

```
blog/portfolio/themes/basic/static/css/style.css
.pagination > .page-item.active {
  background-color: #333;
}

.pagination > .page-item.active > .page-link {
  color: #fff;
}

.pagination > .page-item.disabled > .page-link {
  color: #ddd;
}
```

View the posts page, and this time you'll see styled pagination:

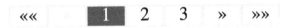

Now that you know the pagination works, open themes/basic/layouts/posts/list.html and change the number of paginated results to 10 posts:

```
{{ range (.Paginator 10).Pages }}
```

Alternatively, since the default is 10, change the range line back to the original code:

```
{{ range .Paginator.Pages }}
```

You can then control the number of results globally in the site's configuration by adding the Paginate field to config.toml:

```
Paginate = 10
```

With pagination in place, your blog list pages will be more manageable for your visitors. Now let's add interactivity to your blog posts with comments.

Adding Comments to Posts Using Disqus

Many blogs include a commenting system that lets your community of readers interact with your posts. Hugo only generates static sites, but you can add support for comments using Disqus,[5] a platform that hosts comments and provides tools for community moderation. Hugo has built-in support for Disqus. To use it, you'll create a Disqus account for your site, set the site name in your Hugo site's configuration file, and include the Disqus template on your pages.

---

5.   https://disqus.com

Handling Lots of Posts

Once you've been adding new content to your site consistently, or if you've migrated content into your site, you'll end up with hundreds of files in your 'posts' folder, which can be difficult to manage.

Hugo uses the folders that you create inside of your 'content' folder to define content sections, but you can create subfolders within these folders to organize your content in a way that works better for you. For example, you can create a '2020' folder inside 'posts' and move all of the posts from 2020 into that folder. Hugo will still see them as posts.

By default, Hugo tries to mirror what's on disk with how the URLs are constructed, but you can override that with the 'url' front matter field on each document or with the 'permalinks' configuration settings like you did in [xxx](#sec.customizing.url.posts).

You can explore content sections in more detail, including how to create nested content sections, in Hugo's documentation.[a]

---

a.   https://gohugo.io/content-management/sections/

Create a new account on Disqus for your site. Once your account is created, select the option to use Disqus on your site. Disqus will ask you to provide a few pieces of info about your site:

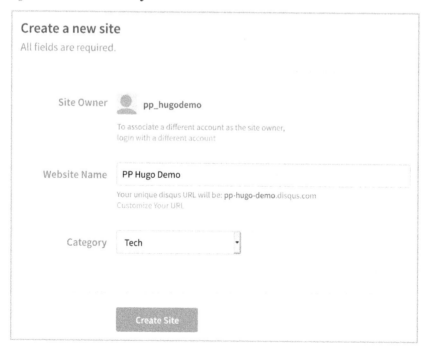

Fill in the name of your site and select the appropriate category. Take note of the URL that Disqus shows under the Website Name field; you'll need the first part, which Disqus calls the "shortname," to link your Hugo site to Disqus. In the preceding image, the URL for the site is pp-hugo-demo.disqus.com, so the shortname is pp-hugo-demo. Press the Create Site button to continue.

Next, select a plan. You can pay for Disqus or use the free ad-supported tier.

Once you've selected your plan, you're presented with options to integrate Disqus with your site. Scroll to the bottom and choose the option to set up Disqus manually. This presents you with some code snippets you can add to your website. You can ignore this, as you'll use Hugo's built-in Disqus template shortly. Continue to the Configure Disqus option.

The Configure Disqus page lets you fill in the website URL, the description, and a few other attributes. You don't need to fill these in now either. Press the Complete Setup button.

Then, open config.toml and add the following line to tell Hugo the shortname for the Disqus site you configured:

```
blog/portfolio/config.toml
theme = "basic"
➤ disqusShortname = "pp-hugo-demo"
```

In this example, the shortname is pp-hugo-demo. Save the file and then stop the Hugo server and restart it again, just to make sure the new setting is applied.

Next, open the blog post layout at themes/basic/layout/posts/single.html, and after the article contents, add a new comments section that uses Hugo's built-in Disqus template:

```
blog/portfolio/themes/basic/layouts/posts/single.html
    <section class="body">
      {{ .Content }}
    </section>
➤   <section class="comments">
➤     <h3>Comments</h3>
➤     {{ template "_internal/disqus.html" . }}
➤   </section>
```

This template uses the disqusShortname shortname variable you set in config.toml and pulls in the Disqus commenting interface for this page. Save the file.

As it turns out, Disqus won't load if your site is served from the localhost domain, so you won't be able to see it in action. To get around this, you have a few different options:

- Host the site via a fully qualified domain name.

- Edit your local hosts file and create an entry like example.com that points to your local machine. Then visit http://example.com:1313 in your browser.

- Use a tunneling service and its client to proxy connections through external servers.

We'll use the last approach, as it also offers an easy way to share your work with others while you're developing your site. The service localtunnel.me[6] is a free service that lets you do this quickly using their command-line client. The client is written in Node.js, which means you need Node installed on your local machine.

Use the npx command, included with Node.js, to launch the localtunnel client and proxy your site. Ensure the Hugo server is running, open a new Terminal window, and execute this command:

```
$ npx localtunnel -p 1313
npx: installed 55 in 3.292s
your url is: https://grumpy-turtle-68.localtunnel.me
```

This downloads the localtunnel package and executes its binary. The -p flag specifies on which port your development server is running.

Use the URL you see in your terminal to access your site. Visit one of your posts and you'll see your Disqus comments section at the bottom of the page:

Third Post

By Brian Hogan

Posted January 1, 2020 in software html

Reading time: 0 minutes.

Lorem ipsum dolor sit amet, consectetur adipisicing elit, sed do eiusmod tempor incididunt ut labore et dolore magna aliqua.

Ut enim ad minim veniam, quis nostrud exercitation ullamco laboris nisi ut aliquip ex ea commodo consequat.

Comments

0 Comments   PP Hugo Demo   🛈 pp_hugodemo ▾

♡ Recommend   🐦 Tweet   f Share   Sort by Best ▾

        Start the discussion…

---

6.   https://localtunnel.me

As it stands now, you've added comments to every blog post. However, you might occasionally want to disallow comments on a page.

Open the first-post.md file and add a new piece of front matter that turns comments off:

```
blog/portfolio/content/posts/first-post.md
categories:
- Personal
- Thoughts
tags:
- software
- html
➤ disableComments: true
```

Then, modify the post layout to use this value to determine whether or not the comments should display:

```
blog/portfolio/themes/basic/layouts/posts/single.html
   <section class="comments">
     <h3>Comments</h3>
➤    {{ if .Params.disableComments }}
➤      <p>Comments are disabled for this post</p>
➤    {{ else }}
➤      {{ template "_internal/disqus.html" . }}
➤    {{ end }}
```

Return to your browser and visit the "First Post" page; you'll see that comments are disabled for that page. Visit one of the other posts to ensure that you can still comment there. When you deploy your site to production, visitors will be able to comment and discuss your content, but only on the posts you choose. Remember to use Disqus's interface to manage and moderate the comments people leave on your site though.

Switch to the terminal window that's running the localtunnel server and use Ctrl+c to shut it down. You can then close the terminal window as you won't need it anymore.

Your blog is almost complete. Let's add one final feature: showing people other posts related to the one they're reading.

Displaying Related Content

When people find a page on your site through a social media share or a search result, you might want to make some of your other content visible as well. Hugo lets you display related content and has some sensible defaults for doing so. To enable this feature, you have to add some keywords to your pages' front matter section. You also have to add some code to your single page template that displays the related content. To demonstrate, let's add a keywords section to the front matter of the Jabberwocky project and the second-post blog post.

First, open content/projects/jabberwocky.md and add the keywords section. Like tags, it's a list:

```
blog/portfolio/content/projects/jabberwocky.md
tech_used:
- JavaScript
- CSS
- HTML
➤ keywords:
➤ - jabberwocky
```

Add the same keywords section to content/posts/second-post.md:

```
blog/portfolio/content/posts/second-post.md
tags:
- software
- html
➤ keywords:
➤ - jabberwocky
```

Then, open themes/basic/layouts/posts/single.html and add this code below your post but above the comments section:

```
blog/portfolio/themes/basic/layouts/posts/single.html
    <section class="body">
      {{ .Content }}
    </section>

➤   <section class="related">
➤     {{ $related := .Site.RegularPages.Related . | first 5 }}
➤     {{ with $related }}
➤       <h3>Related pages</h3>
➤       <ul>
➤         {{ range . }}
➤         <li><a href="{{ .RelPermalink }}">{{ .Title }}</a></li>
➤         {{ end }}
➤       </ul>
➤     {{ end }}
➤   </section>
```

This code uses a with block to check if there's any related content. If there is, it displays the header and the list of content.

By adding the same keyword to the Jabberwocky project and the "second post" blog post, the Jabberwocky project now shows up as a related piece of content as shown in the screenshot on page 77.

> **Second Post**
>
> By Brian Hogan
>
> Posted January 1, 2020 in software html
>
> Reading time: 0 minutes.
>
> Lorem ipsum dolor sit amet, consectetur adipisicing elit, sed do eiusmod tempor incididunt ut labore et dolore magna aliqua.
>
> Ut enim ad minim veniam, quis nostrud exercitation ullamco laboris nisi ut aliquip ex ea commodo consequat.
>
> **Related pages**
>
> - Jabberwocky

This is a great way to make people aware of your work. Add keywords throughout your pages to get them to show up on your blog posts.

Hugo uses these default settings for related content, creating indices on the keywords and dates of your content:

```
[related]
threshold = 80.0
includeNewer = false
toLower = false

  [[related.indices]]
  name = "keywords"
  weight = 100.0

  [[related.indices]]
  name = "date"
  weight = 10.0
```

To change the behavior of related content, you must add the entire configuration block to your config.toml file and then modify it to suit your needs.

There are a few options you might want to explore when setting up the related post content. For example, the includeNewer option, if set to true, will update older pages on your site with new related content. The threshold is a number between 0 and 100, with lower numbers showing more content with less relevance. Also, the toLower option can increase the matches by lowercasing the keywords and queries that get created for finding related content.

You can also add new indices for tags, author, or any other front matter fields for that matter. The weight for each index you create controls how relevant this index is compared to others. Experiment with these values to get the right balance for your content.

Your Turn

Before moving on to the next chapter, complete the following tasks:

1. Create a layout for the tag pages using the same approach you used for year and month pages. Create the tag list template in themes/basic/layouts/_default/tags.html.

2. Create layouts for the /categories page and the individual category pages.

3. Add an optional header image for your blog posts. Images go in the static folder, and you link to them using the same approach you use when you link your CSS files. Use front matter to define the banner image for a post and display it if it exists.

4. Apply pagination to your project list.

5. Place your latest blog post on the home page of your site.

Wrapping Up

You've applied what you learned about creating content sections and data to build a blog. You've gained a few new skills as well. You know how to customize URLs for sections of your site, you can organize content using taxonomies, and you can add comments using Disqus to your pages.

With all this new content, you'll need a way for people to find it. So let's look at how you can integrate search into your site.

CHAPTER 6

Adding Search to Your Site

Once you've created a large amount of content on your site, you'll want to make it easier for people to find things. When your site is live for all the world to see, you'll want to make sure everyone can find your content.

You'll also want a local search engine for your site, especially for situations where you have a significantly large corpus of content.

Database-driven sites like WordPress have built-in search capabilities. When a visitor seearches for content, their keywords are used to build a query that gets sent to the database containing the content. The database returns results that match, and the system displays the page.

For static sites like Hugo, you're working without a database, so you're going to have to think about solving the problem differently. You can use a third-party search service like Algolia,[1] which indexes your content and lets you search it. You can set up your own search indexer like ElasticSearch[2] and integrate it into your site. Or you can generate your own search index and use client-side JavaScript to perform the search.

In this chapter, we'll take the last approach. You'll build a client-side search engine using a JavaScript library called Lunr[3] to do the heavy lifting. Lunr needs a list of your site's content in JSON format, so you'll leverage Hugo's ability to generate JSON to create that list.

1. https://www.algolia.com
2. https://www.elastic.co
3. https://lunrjs.com

Creating the Document Collection

For Lunr to search your site, it needs to know about all of the documents available, and it'll need the titles and some text to search. Lunr accepts a collection of documents that looks something like this:

```
[{
  "name": "A document",
  "text": "A bunch of content filled with amazing thoughts."
}, {
  "name": "A second document",
  "text": "Similar, but different from the first one."
}]
```

To generate the search index that Lunr needs, you'll use an approach similar to how you generated the projects JSON feed; you'll create a layout for the search index that iterates through all of the pages in the site, emitting the fields that Lunr will use. Later, you'll fetch this JSON file from the server using JavaScript, parse it with Lunr, and match it against the search terms your visitor provides.

Create the file themes/basic/layouts/_default/search.json and add the following code which iterates through all the pages in the site and displays the title, the body, and the link to the page:

```
search/portfolio/themes/basic/layouts/_default/search.json
{
  "results": [
    {{- range $index, $page := .Site.RegularPages }}
    {{- if $index -}} , {{- end }}
    {
      "href": {{ .Permalink | jsonify }},
      "title": {{ .Title | jsonify }},
      "body": {{ .Content | plainify | jsonify }}
    }
    {{- end }}
  ]
}
```

The .RegularPages collection gives you access to all of the pages on the site. You'll need the link to the page when you eventually display the search results to the visitor.

Next, create the Search content page itself. It won't have any content, but you need it so you can specify the output formats. Define both an HTML and JSON format, as you'll create an HTML layout which will display the actual search interface shortly.

Create content/search.md:

```
$ hugo new search.md
/Users/brianhogan/portfolio/content/search.md created
```

Modify the file's front matter so it displays the output formats. Use layout to associate this file with the search layout you created, and make sure draft is set to false:

search/portfolio/content/search.md

```
---
title: "Search"
date: 2020-01-02T12:42:17-05:00
draft: false
➤ outputs:
➤ - HTML
➤ - JSON
➤ layout: search
---
```

Save the file. This is enough to generate the search index. Start the Hugo server and visit http://localhost:1313/search/index.json and you'll see your documents:

```
{
  "results": [
    {
      "href": "http://localhost:1313/search/",
      "title": "Search",
      "body": ""
    },
    {
      "href": "http://localhost:1313/posts/2020/01/third-post/",
      "title": "Third Post",
      "body": "Lorem ipsum dolor sit amet, consectetur adipisicing elit, sed
              do eiusmod tempor incididunt ut labore et dolore magna aliqua.\n
              Ut enim ad minim veniam, quis nostrud exercitation ullamco
              laboris nisi ut aliquip ex ea commodo consequat.\n"
    },

  ...

    {
      "href": "http://localhost:1313/projects/linkitivity/",
      "title": "Linkitivity",
      "body": "Description of the Linkitivity project\u0026hellip;\n"
    }
  ]
}
```

You now have a single JSON file that contains the entire contents of your site. Let's build the page that displays the search box next.

Joe asks:

Won't the Search Index Get Huge If I Have a Lot of Content?

Yes it will. And a large JSON file will take longer for your visitors to download and longer for Lunr to index. You might consider using the summary instead of the entire content. This will reduce the size of the file, but will also reduce the reliability of your searches, as they'll have less to work with. In that case you can explore other options. On a site like this, a single search index such as this one won't cause any serious performance issues. On sites with thousands of pages, a solution like Algolia will probably be a better fit.

Creating the Search Interface

Right now, when you visit http://localhost/search in your browser, you see the title. The search.md file you created renders output in both JSON and HTML formats, but you only created a JSON layout. The default single page layout is currently applied, but you didn't define any content in the search.md file. Let's get the search form to appear on the page.

Create the file themes/basic/layouts/_default/search.html and add the following code, which defines the main block, displays the title, and defines a text box, button, and area for search results:

search/portfolio/themes/basic/layouts/_default/search.html
```
{{ define "main" }}

  <h2>{{ .Title }}</h2>

  <input type="search" id="searchField">
  <button id="searchButton">Search</button>

  <div id="output">
    <p>Waiting for search input</p>
  </div>
{{ end }}
```

Save the file. Visit http://localhost:1313/search in your browser and you'll see the form as shown in the screenshot on page 83.

At this point, the form doesn't do anything. To implement the search functionality, you need to write some JavaScript and attach it to this page. You'll fetch the document collection you just created, use the Lunr library to build a search index from that document collection, and perform a search using the text your visitor submits.

Search

	Search

Waiting for search input

You'll use the Axios[4] library to fetch remote data. Axios is a promise-based library that makes grabbing remote data a breeze.

To use Lurn and Axios, you need to include them on your page. Open themes/basic/layouts/_default/search.html and, right before the {{ end }} markup, add these two lines to load the Lunr and Axios JavaScript libraries from a Content Delivery Network (CDN):

search/portfolio/themes/basic/layouts/_default/search.html
```
<script src="//unpkg.com/lunr@2.3.6/lunr.js"></script>
<script src="//unpkg.com/axios@0.19.0/dist/axios.js"></script>
```

Using a CDN saves you the trouble of downloading them locally, and lets you take advantage of the caching mechanisms the CDN provides. In the next chapter, you'll refactor this to use npm and Webpack to create a bundle that contains these libraries, so you won't be relying on the CDN. But let's get the search working first before adding additional complexity.

Create the file themes/basic/static/js/search.js and add an alert statement to the file so you can test that the script loads properly:

```
alert("Search!");
```

Save the file, and then switch back to themes/basic/layouts/_default/search.html and include the search.js file by adding this code after the other script tags:

search/portfolio/themes/basic/layouts/_default/search.html
```
<script src="{{ "js/search.js" | relURL }}"></script>
```

Now, visit https://localhost:1313/search and you'll see an alert box pop up. This demonstrates that your JavaScript is properly linked up.

Switch back to themes/basic/static/js/search.js. Remove the alert line from the file.

Define a global SearchApp object, which will hold some references you'll need throughout the search script:

---

4.   https://github.com/axios/axios

```
search/portfolio/themes/basic/static/js/search.js
'use strict'
window.SearchApp = {
  searchField: document.getElementById("searchField"),
  searchButton: document.getElementById("searchButton"),
  output: document.getElementById("output"),
  searchData: {},
  searchIndex: {}
};
```

This stores references to the search field, search button, and the output area. It also defines two other properties: searchData and searchIndex.

You'll fetch the JSON data from the server and store it in the searchData property. Then you'll feed that to Lunr, which will build a search index that you'll store in searchIndex. You'll need to keep the original JSON data around because when you query the search index, the list of results won't contain the title and other information in the search index. The results you'll get contain the hyperlink to the page, along with other data like the relevance and weight. To display the page title, you'll cross-reference the results you get with the original data.

Use the Axios library to fetch the data from the search page. When you get the results, store them in the searchData property. Then populate the search index with the results from the field:

```
search/portfolio/themes/basic/static/js/search.js
axios
  .get('/search/index.json')
  .then(response => {
    SearchApp.searchData = response.data;
    SearchApp.searchIndex = lunr(function () {
      this.ref('href');
      this.field('title');
      this.field('body');
      response.data.results.forEach(e => {
        this.add(e);
      });
    });
  });
```

Lunr uses the data from the title and the body to build the search index. When you perform a search, Lunr will compare the search terms with the words in its index and generate results.

Next, add an event listener to the search button which calls a search function, and then implement the function which uses Lunr to perform the search:

search/portfolio/themes/basic/static/js/search.js

```
SearchApp.searchButton.addEventListener('click', search);

function search() {
  let searchText = SearchApp.searchField.value;

  let resultList = SearchApp.searchIndex.search(searchText);

  let list = [];
  let results = resultList.map(entry => {
    SearchApp.searchData.results.filter(d => {
      if(entry.ref == d.href) {
        list.push(d);
      }
    })
  });

  display(list);

}
```

Lunr gives you results, but the results only contain a score and a hyperlink.
To get results you can display, search through the JSON data you pulled from
the server and match on the URLs. Then call the display function to display
the results you found.

Finally, write the display function, which iterates over the results and displays
them:

search/portfolio/themes/basic/static/js/search.js

```
function display(list) {

  SearchApp.output.innerText = '';
  if (list.length > 0) {
    const ul = document.createElement("ul");
    list.forEach(el => {
      const li = document.createElement("li");
      const a = document.createElement("a");
      a.href = el.href;
      a.text = el.title;
      li.appendChild(a);
      ul.appendChild(li);
    });

    SearchApp.output.appendChild(ul);
  }else{
    SearchApp.output.innerHTML = "Nothing found";
  }

};
```

Take the search out for a spin. This current implementation only finds whole words, so search for "Jabberwocky" and you'll see the link to that project appear in the results.

Search

```
jabberwocky|                        Search
```

  • Jabberwocky

Let's tweak the search to make it a little more useful.

Improving the Search

When you pass text to Lunr, it's turning the text into a search query. When you pass single words, it searches for all documents containing that word. But if you search for multiple words, Lunr defaults to searching for documents that contain either word. So a search for "first post" would return all the documents with the word "first" or the word "post".

If you wanted to show documents that contain all of the words, you'd have to place plus signs in front of each word. For example, to find pages with "first post", you'd have to search for +first +post.

Finally, Lunr supports partial word search. You can use wildcard characters. Search for jabber* and you'll get the result you're looking for.

Your visitors won't know about these search capabilities unless you add instructions to the site, so let's modify the behavior of the search to make it easier for people to use. You'll add asterisks to each word, and then add a checkbox that specifies that you're looking for all words. If it's checked, you'll change the query yourself.

Add the wildcards first. Take the value you get from the search form, use the split() function to turn it into an array of words, use the map() function to transform each word and append the asterisk to each word, and then use join() to convert the result back to a string:

search/portfolio/themes/basic/static/js/search.js
```
function search() {
  let searchText = SearchApp.searchField.value;

➤   searchText = searchText
➤     .split(" ")
➤     .map( word => { return word + "*" })
➤     .join(" ");
```

Save the file. Then try out the search in your browser by searching for Fir. The "First Post" entry displays.

When you use asterisks, Lunr will no longer find some complete words. If you search for "Jabberwocky" now, it won't return any results because using wildcards disables Lunr's *stemming* support. Stemming[5] is the process of reducing a word to its stem. For example, if you have the words "building" or "builder", the stem would be "build". Lunr uses stemming to reduce the size of the index it builds. You can disable stemming support by removing it from the pipeline when you create the Lunr index:

search/portfolio/themes/basic/static/js/search.js
```
SearchApp.searchIndex = lunr(function () {
➤    this.pipeline.remove(lunr.stemmer);
➤    this.searchPipeline.remove(lunr.stemmer);
     this.ref('href');
     this.field('title');
     this.field('body');
     response.data.results.forEach(e => {
       this.add(e);
     });
});
```

Let's add a checkbox to the form to allow users to require that all words are included in the search, instead of the default behavior. First, add a new checkbox field and corresponding label to the form. Open themes/basic/layouts/_default/search.html and add the new field:

search/portfolio/themes/basic/layouts/_default/search.html
```
<input type="search" id="searchField">
<button id="searchButton">Search</button>
➤ <input id="allwords" type="checkbox">
➤ <label for="allwords">Require all words</label>
```

Switch back to themes/basic/static/js/search.js and add a new field to the searchApp object that references the new checkbox:

search/portfolio/themes/basic/static/js/search.js
```
window.SearchApp = {
  searchField: document.getElementById("searchField"),
  searchButton: document.getElementById("searchButton"),
➤  allwords: document.getElementById("allwords"),
  output: document.getElementById("output"),
  searchData: {},
  searchIndex: {}
};
```

---

5.   https://lunrjs.com/guides/core_concepts.html#stemming

Finally, in the search() function, right before you perform the search, check the checkbox. If it's checked, prepend each word with a plus sign, using the same technique you used to append asterisks for the wildcards:

search/portfolio/themes/basic/static/js/search.js

```
if (SearchApp.allwords.checked) {
  searchText = searchText
  .split(" ")
    .map( word => { return "+" + word })
    .join(" ");
}

let resultList = SearchApp.searchIndex.search(searchText);
```

Save the file. Back in your browser, enter "first post" in the field, select the checkbox, and search. "First Post" is now the only result. Uncheck the box and you'll get different results:

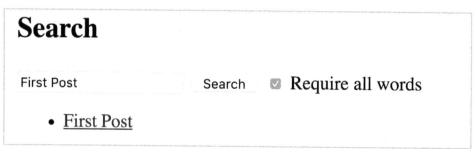

The order in which Lunr displays results is based on how many times the word appears in the document. When you perform the search, Lunr returns each result, along with a score. The more times a word appears, the higher the score. You can use these scores to set thresholds and tune your search even further.

Your Turn

Here are some additional things for you to explore to make your search more robust:

1. If you enter nothing in the search field, all the pages come back in the results. Modify the code to handle blank searches.

2. Some of the content of your pages is hidden in front matter. For example, your project pages contain technology used, which you might want to see in your searches. Explore how you can include this data in addition to the title and body content.

3. Review the Lunr documentation to explore how to create a serialized search index instead of creating one on the client. This will require additional processing when you publish your site, but it will speed things up substantially if you have a lot of content.

4. Explore other search options like Algolia and see how they stack up compared to Lunr.

Wrapping Up

You added a basic search to your site, using Hugo to generate a catalog of content, and JavaScript to download and search it. You refined the search to take advantage of some of Lunr's features. In the next chapter, you'll use Hugo's asset management features to process your CSS and JavaScript files, getting things one step closer to production.

CHAPTER 7

Managing Assets with Pipes

A website is more than just its content. Stylesheets, images, and JavaScript bring a site to life, but managing these assets can be tricky.

When you're getting your site ready for production, you're looking for ways to make the experience better for your visitors. To improve speed, it's common practice to process CSS and JavaScript files to *minify* them, which involves removing whitespace, line breaks, and comments to reduce the file size so the files transfer faster. It's also common to *fingerprint* the CSS and JavaScript files so that they'll have slightly different filenames when you deploy modified versions. This invalidates browser caches so visitors see your changes.

You might even want to take advantage of Sass, a CSS preprocessor that lets you break up your stylesheets, add logic, and create shared functionality. And now that you have a JS-powered search, you might want to create a bundle for your JavaScript files instead of relying on a version hosted by a CDN.

Hugo can handle all of this out of the box, thanks to its Pipes feature. Pipes let you transform your CSS and other assets right from within Hugo. You won't need to install additional tooling to concatenate, minify, or fingerprint your files. As long as you've installed the extended version of Hugo, you've got everything you need.

Hugo also includes some powerful built-in features for managing images, including the ability to resize images automatically, or perform other forms of image processing, without the need for external tooling.

In this chapter, you'll use Hugo's built-in features to manage your CSS, images, and JavaScript files. You'll also integrate Webpack[1] into your project so that you can take advantage of advanced features Hugo doesn't support,

---

1.   https://webpack.js.org/

such as JavaScript modules. And since you're going to do that integration, you'll create some scripts to make building your project easier.

Managing Stylesheets

Right now you have a single CSS file for the site with a pretty minimalist design. As it grows, you may want to break it up into components, or evolve it further.

To use the pipelines feature of Hugo, you'll need to move your CSS files out of the static directory and into a new assets directory.

Stop your Hugo server with Ctrl-c. Create a new directory in your theme named assets. You can do this with your editor, or with the following command:

```
$ mkdir themes/basic/assets
```

Then move the static/css directory there:

```
$ mv themes/basic/static/css themes/basic/assets
```

Then in themes/basic/layouts/partials/head.html, locate the line of code that loads the stylesheet. Add this line above the stylesheet link to load the assets/css/style.css file:

```
➤    {{ $css := resources.Get "css/style.css" }}
     <link rel="stylesheet" href="{{ "css/style.css" | relURL }}">
```

The resources.Get function uses the assets directory as its base path. The contents of the file are read in to the $css variable.

To use the CSS file, modify the stylesheet link to use the $css variable:

```
<link rel="stylesheet" href="{{ $css.RelPermalink }}">
```

The $css.RelPermalink piece writes the file to your site's public/css/ directory and places the proper relative URL into the HTML document.

Start your server with hugo server and visit your home page again to ensure your styles still work.

Now that you're pulling the CSS in with resources.Get, you can apply some transformations to the file.

Minifying and Fingerprinting Your CSS

It's common practice to minify front-end content. This removes non-printable characters and comments, resulting in smaller files that transfer faster.

In addition, you can fingerprint your assets. When you serve up your stylesheet, your browser will cache it. When you update the page, your browser might not notice the changes unless you clear your local cache. One way to get around that is by using fingerprinting to create a unique filename for your CSS files that gets updated every time you make changes.

Hugo supports both minification and fingerprinting when you use the resources.Get function. You can pipe the resource to the minify and fingerprint functions. Modify the resources.Get line to do just that:

```
{{ $css := resources.Get "css/style.css" | minify | fingerprint }}
<link rel="stylesheet" href="{{ "css/style.css" | relURL }}">
```

This results in a file with a name like /css/style.min.a939605b22...815d1.css". Its contents are minified, and the filename will change when you change the contents. Because Hugo is managing all of this, you don't have to think about it.

Using Sass

Sass is a CSS preprocessor that offers advanced features. With Sass, you can break up your CSS into manageable chunks, define variables, and perform math. While some of these features are making their way into browsers, Sass is a popular choice for building front-end sites.

First, rename themes/basic/assets/css/style.css to themes/basic/assets/css.style.scss:

```
$ mv themes/basic/assets/css/style.css themes/basic/assets/css/style.scss
```

The scss syntax of Sass is a superset of CSS, so a CSS file is already a valid Sass file.

To use this file, update the filename and introduce the toCSS function into the pipeline, in front of the minify function:

```
assets/portfolio/themes/basic/layouts/partials/head.html
{{ $css := resources.Get "css/style.scss" | toCSS | minify | fingerprint }}
```

This gets things working, and you can now integrate many of Sass's features into your styles.

For a quick example, let's extract the styles for the navbar into its own file so it'll be easier to manage.

Create the file themes/basic/assets/css/_navbar.scss. The underscore denotes that this is a Sass partial which you can include into a main Sass stylesheet.

Switch to styles.scss and locate the styles related to the navigation bar:

```
nav {
  display: flex;
  flex-direction: column;
}
```

```
nav > a {
  flex: 1;
  text-align: center;
  text-decoration: none;
  color: #fff;
}
```

Remember that one of the styles for the navigation bar is within a media query with some other styles:

```
@media only screen and (min-width: 768px) {
  nav { flex-direction: row; }

  .project-container { display: flex; }

  .project-container .project-list { width: 20%; }

  .project-container .project { flex: 1; }
}
```

Cut these style rules from the file and paste them into the _navbar.scss file. Create a new media query also. Your file will look like this when you're done:

assets/portfolio/themes/basic/assets/css/_navbar.scss
```
nav {
  display: flex;
  flex-direction: column;
}

nav > a {
  flex: 1;
  text-align: center;
  text-decoration: none;
  color: #fff;
}

@media only screen and (min-width: 768px) {
  nav { flex-direction: row; }
}
```

Then, back in the style.scss file, add an import statement, which will pull the _navbar.scss file's contents into the main stylesheet when Hugo builds your site:

assets/portfolio/themes/basic/assets/css/style.scss
```
nav, footer {
  background-color: #333;
  color: #fff;
  text-align: center;
}
```
➤ `@import 'navbar';`

Save all of your changes. You now have a path forward to creating more complex and organized stylesheets for your site.

You haven't done too much with images in this book yet, but that's about to change. Hugo has some fantastic features for working with images that you'll explore next.

Managing Images

Up until now, you've used placeholder images in your pages, but you're going to want to place images in your blog posts, or screenshots of your projects. And you might even want an image on your home page. Hugo offers a few options for managing images: you can host images externally and link to them, you can place them in the static folder like you did with CSS files, or you can create a resource bundle and keep images with their associated content.

You already brought in images from an external site in Chapter 3, Adding Content Sections, on page 25. If your images are hosted elsewhere, you can use that same approach.

To link to images in the static folder of your theme or your site, use a standard <img> tag with a site-relative URL. This works in both your layouts and in your Markdown content.

Test this out by adding a local image to your site's footer. In the companion files for this book, you'll find an images directory. Copy the hugo-logo-wide.svg file from that directory to your site's static directory. You could also place it in the static directory within your theme. Either way, you'll access the file the same way, as the static directories are merged together.

With the file in place, open your theme's footer partial at themes/basic/layouts/partials/footer.html and add the following code to include the image with a link to the official Hugo website:

```
assets/portfolio/themes/basic/layouts/partials/footer.html
<footer>
  <small>Copyright {{now.Format "2006"}} Me.</small>
  <p>Powered by<br>
    <a href="https://gohugo.io">
      <img src="{{ "hugo-logo-wide.svg" | relURL }}" width="128" height="38">
    </a>
  </p>
</footer>
```

Even though the image is located at /static/hugo-logo-wide.svg, you don't specify the static part of the path to the file, as the contents of the static folder are copied to the root of the site. Using the relURL function ensures that the paths are generated relative to the page.

Save the file. When you load the page in your browser, the Hugo logo appears in the footer:

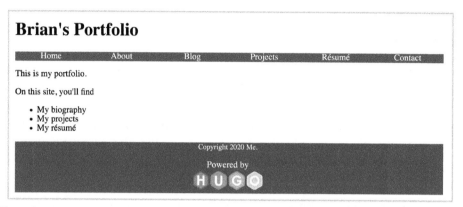

If you're going to store more images in the static folder, you'll probably want better organization. Create an images folder to store your images, and then include images in your image paths.

Images in the static folder are available in your content pages as well. When you're working in Markdown documents, you include an image using Markdown's image syntax like this:

```
![Text description of image](/path/to/image.png)
```

However, if you're going to include images in your Markdown content, Hugo has a better way, which will give you access to powerful functions to transform images: page bundles.

Using Page Bundles to Organize Content

Up until now, each piece of content you've created is a Markdown file with a name that somewhat resembles its title. But you can also create a page bundle, which is a collection of content files, including images, PDF files, or any other type of asset you want to keep close to your content. A page bundle is a folder inside of your content section, rather than an individual file.

To test this out, add a fourth blog post to your site. This post will contain a few images in addition to the text, and by using a page bundle, you'll be able to keep those images in the same location as the text, making the content easier to organize.

Use the hugo new command to create the page bundle:

```
$ hugo new posts/my-vacation/index.md
/Users/brianhogan/portfolio/content/posts/my-vacation/index.md created
```

Notice that instead of calling the post my-vacation.md, you're specifying my-vacation as part of the path, and specifying a file named index.md. Hugo creates the following structure:

```
content/posts/
├── first-post.md
├── my-vacation
│   └── index.md
├── second-post.md
└── third-post.md
```

This new my-vacation folder is where all of the assets associated with your post will go. Create a new images folder inside of this folder using your IDE or the following Terminal command:

```
$ mkdir content/posts/my-vacation/images
```

In the companion files you downloaded for this book, you'll find three photos in the images folder: badlands.jpg, rushmore.jpg, and bison.jpg. Copy all three of these photos to the content/posts/my-vacation/images folder.

Open portfolio/content/posts/my-vacation/index.md and add the following content:

```
assets/portfolio/content/posts/my-vacation/index.md
---
title: "My Vacation"
date: 2020-01-02T12:45:51-06:00
draft: false
author: Brian Hogan
categories:
- Personal
tags:
- family
year: "2020"
month: "2020/01"

---
Here are pictures from my recent trip to South Dakota.
```

Now, include one of the images in your document. But instead of using a regular <img> tag, you'll use a <figure> tag, which lets you associate an image with a caption. Here's what that might look like, but don't add this code to your page, as Hugo doesn't support raw HTML code in Markdown documents:

```
<figure>
  <img src="images/rushmore.jpg" width="600"> <figcaption>
    <h4>Mount Rushmore</h4>
  </figcaption>
</figure>
```

Instead of typing that code, you'll use a *shortcode*, which is a way for you to extend Hugo's Markdown capabilities. Shortcodes are functions powered by Go's templating mechanism that you can use in your Markdown. You call them and pass them options, and they generate output. Hugo has built-in shortcodes for adding code snippets, YouTube videos, and of course, figures. Add this code to your file:

```
{{< figure src="images/rushmore.jpg" width="600"
           alt="Mount Rushmore" title="Mount Rushmore" >}}
```

This generates the <figure> element, the caption, and the alternative text just as if you'd entered them manually.

The image you've added is quite large, though. You'll tackle that properly in the next section. For now, add a CSS rule for images inside of figures that resizes the images appropriately for different devices:

```
assets/portfolio/themes/basic/assets/css/style.scss
figure img {
  max-width: 100%;
  height: auto;
}
```

With this style rule in place, the image will stay within the container:

Here are pictures from my recent trip to South Dakota.

Mount Rushmore

It will also scale down on smaller screens:

Here are pictures from my recent trip to
South Dakota.

Mount Rushmore

Hugo's built-in shortcodes are great for incorporating assets into your posts, but you can write your own shortcodes to have even more control over your assets.

Using a Shortcode to Process Images

When you're working with images for the web, you often need to resize them so they're smaller, or perform other processing tasks. Hugo has built-in methods for altering images, provided they're defined as *page resources*. Anything in your page bundle is automatically a page resource, so that means Hugo can manipulate the images you've copied into the my-vacation folder.

In a nutshell, Hugo makes it possible to do something like this with an image:

```
{{ $image := $.Page.Resources.Get("path/to/image.jpg")}}
{{ $smallImage := $image.Resize "1024x" }}
<img src="{{ $smallImage }}" width="{{ $smallImage.Width }}"
                        height="{{ $smallImage.Height }}">
```

When Hugo builds your site, it creates a new resized image, rather than the original high-resolution one you supplied. There are many other image processing functions[2] for resampling, cropping, and fitting images into your pages. In addition, there are other image functions[3] that let you control brightness, gamma, contrast, and color.

Unfortunately, you can't take advantage of these features directly in your content pages, as their functionality is only available within Hugo's layouts.

---

2. https://gohugo.io/content-management/image-processing/
3. https://gohugo.io/functions/images/

To get around that, you can create your own shortcodes. Shortcodes let you do things in your Markdown content that you'd normally only be able to do in your layouts. With a shortcode, you can use conditional logic, page variables, and of course, process images. To create your own shortcode, create a shortcodes directory in the layouts directory of your theme or site, create an HTML file with the name of the shortcode, and write the code that you want to execute when you invoke the shortcode in your Markdown.

Let's create a shortcode called postimage that will accept an image and some alternative text. It'll generate a <figure> element with a caption. It'll automatically resize the image, but also create a link to the original image, so your readers can access the larger image by clicking the smaller version.

First, create a shortcodes directory in the layouts dfirectory of your theme. The following terminal command can do that for you:

```
$ mkdir themes/basic/layouts/shortcodes
```

Then, create the file themes/basic/layouts/shortcodes/postimage.html and add the following code to get a reference to an image and create a smaller version of the image:

```
assets/portfolio/themes/basic/layouts/shortcodes/postimage.html
{{ $image := $.Page.Resources.GetMatch (.Get 0)}}
{{ $smallImage := $image.Resize "1024x" }}
```

The (.Get 0) piece gives you access to the first argument, which will be the image's filename. Once you have the image reference, you create the smaller version using the .Resize function. Passing the width only will tell Hugo to keep the aspect ratio of the image so that you won't end up with a distorted image or have to determine the aspect ratio yourself.

Now, add this code to create the figure element with the hyperlink, image tag, and caption:

```
assets/portfolio/themes/basic/layouts/shortcodes/postimage.html
<figure class="post-figure">
  <a href="{{ $image.RelPermalink }}">
    {{ with $smallImage }}
    <img src="{{ .RelPermalink }}"
         width="{{ .Width }}" height="{{ .Height }}"
         alt="{{ $.Get 1 }}" />
    {{ end }}
  </a>
  <figcaption>{{ .Get 1 }}</figcaption>
</figure>
```

The .Get 1 piece fetches the second argument passed to the shortcode, which is the text for the caption and the image's alternative text. The {{ with $smallImage }} block switches the context so that you can call the Width and Height functions without having to prefix them each with $smallImage. It's not necessary, but it saves keystrokes. Since the context has changed, you must prefix .Get 1 with a dollar sign ($), so you can reach outside of the current scope.

Save the file and open the blog post again (content/my-vacation/index.md). Replace the existing figure with the shortcode you just created:

```
assets/portfolio/content/posts/my-vacation/index.md
{{< postimage "images/rushmore.jpg" "Mount Rushmore" >}}
```

When you reload the page, you won't see any differences at first, but you can now click each image to see the full-sized version. Hugo performed the smaller version of the image when it generated the page. If you view the page's source, you'll see that it's now referencing both the small and large images:

```
<figure class="post-figure">
  <a href="/posts/2020/01/my-vacation/images/rushmore.jpg">

    <img src="/posts/2020/01/my-vacation/images/rushmore_...resize_q75_box.jpg"
        width="1024" height="686"
        alt="Mount Rushmore" />
  </a>
  <figcaption>Mount Rushmore</figcaption>
</figure>
```

Add the badlands.jpg and bison.jpg images the same way:

```
assets/portfolio/content/posts/my-vacation/index.md
{{< postimage "images/badlands.jpg" "The Badlands" >}}
{{< postimage "images/bison.jpg" "Bison at Custer National Park" >}}
```

Processing images with Hugo can make the build process take considerably longer. To keep things running quickly, Hugo caches the converted images, saving them to the resources folder in the root of your site so that it doesn't have to build them all of the time. However, if you change your settings or sizes, you'll end up with extra files in the resources directory that you no longer need. Use the hugo -gc command to build the site and clean up cached files.

Hugo does a great job of helping you manage your styles and images. Now let's explore how to manage JavaScript files.

Bundling JavaScript Files

When you built the search for your site, you used JavaScript libraries hosted on a CDN. This requires your browser to make additional requests to fetch those libraries. Hugo can combine all of your scripts into a single minified file, and you can fingerprint the file just like you did with your stylesheets.

Sometimes this is preferable, as you'll have all your project's dependencies under your control.

To make this work, first move the js folder from the static directory of your site to the assets directory, just like you've done with stylesheets. You can do this in your editor, or from the command-line interface like this:

```
$ mv themes/basic/static/js themes/basic/assets/js
```

Then, download Lunr and Axios and place them in the assets/js directory, but be sure to grab the full unminified versions. You can use the curl command-line tool to download these files or visit the URLs in your browser and save the files that way:

```
$ cd themes/basic/assets/js
$ curl https://unpkg.com/lunr@2.3.6/lunr.js > lunr.js
$ curl https://unpkg.com/axios@0.19.0/dist/axios.js > axios.js
$ cd -
```

You'll also find these files in the assets/portfolio/themes/basic/assets directory of the book's companion files.

Open themes/basic/layouts/_default/search.html and remove the existing script tags. Replace them with these lines that load Lunr, Axios, and your search.js file:

```
{{ $lunr := resources.Get "js/lunr.js" }}
{{ $axios := resources.Get "js/axios.js" }}
{{ $search := resources.Get "js/search.js" }}
```

The resources.Concat function takes a list of resources (known as a Slice in Go) and combines them into the file you specify. Add these lines to concatenate, minify, and fingerprint the output file:

```
{{ $libs := slice $lunr $axios $search }}
{{ $js := $libs | resources.Concat "js/app.js" | minify | fingerprint }}
<script src="{{ $js.RelPermalink }}"></script>
```

Save the file and restart your Hugo server. Revisit your search page at http://localhost:1313/search and ensure it still works.

Hugo's asset pipeline is a fantastic feature, and you can get pretty far with it, but front-end development can get a lot more complex than concatenation and minification. You'll likely want to use more complex JavaScript build processes for those casses.

Using Webpack and npm with Hugo

Hugo tries hard to draw boundaries between what it does and what other programs should do. While Hugo can minify, concatenate, and fingerprint

JavaScript files, it doesn't have support for more advanced JavaScript development, like import statements and transpilation.

Webpack is one of the most popular tools for managing and building front-end applications. It's powered by Node.js, and as a result, you'll be able to use npm, the package manager for Node.js, to manage all of the dependencies for your project, including Lunr, Axios, and Webpack. You'll also be able to use npm to create a more automated way of building your site.

To get started, create a package.json file. This file lets you track JavaScript dependencies and define tasks to build your site. You can create this file with the npm init command and fill in the details, but it's quicker to create the file manually. First, stop your Hugo server with Ctrl-c.

Create the package.json file in the root of your Hugo project and add the following JSON content to the file:

```
{
  "name": "portfolio",
  "version": "1.0.0",
  "description": "My portfolio",
  "private": true,
  "scripts": {
    "build": "hugo --cleanDestinationDir"
  }
}
```

This specifies the name of the project, the version, and a brief description. The "private": true line ensures you can't accidentally publish your code to a package repository. The "scripts" section lets you specify scripts you'd like to run. This defines a build command that runs Hugo with the --cleanDestinationDir argument, so the public directory is always cleared out.

Save the file, exit your editor, and use npm to build the site. Prefix the name of the script with run, like this:

```
$ npm run build
```

The site builds just like it did before, but now you don't have to remember to add the --cleanDestinationDir option—and you can add additional configuration options here as well.

Add another script that runs the development server with the --disableFastRender option so that nothing gets cached. Be sure to add a comma to the end of the line with the build task or your JSON file won't be valid:

```
"build": "hugo --cleanDestinationDir",
"hugo-server": "hugo server --disableFastRender"
```

Save the file and run the development server:

```
$ npm run hugo-server
```

The server starts up. Press `Ctrl-c` to stop the server.

Now, let's get Webpack working. Add Webpack and its CLI as development dependencies:

```
$ npm install --save-dev webpack webpack-cli
```

While you're installing dependencies, install Lunr and Axios as project dependencies as well. Use the --save flag instead of --save-dev as these are dependencies you'll need for production, not just for development purposes:

```
$ npm install --save axios lunr
```

You can now remove the themes/basic/assets/js/lunr.js and themes/basic/assets/js/axios.js files from your project:

```
$ rm themes/basic/assets/js/lunr.js
$ rm themes/basic/assets/js/axios.js
```

Webpack can use a configuration file that lets you define how it should build your project. Create a webpack.config.js file in the root of your Hugo site. Add this code which looks for an index.js file in themes/basic/assets/js and generates the output in themes/basic/assets/js/app.js:

```
assets/portfolio/webpack.config.js
const path = require('path');

module.exports = {
  entry: './themes/basic/assets/js/index.js',
  output: {
    filename: 'app.js',
    path: path.resolve(__dirname, 'themes','basic','assets', 'js')
  }
};
```

By putting the resulting file in the assets folder, you can still use Hugo's minifier and fingerprinter. If, however, you plan to use other Webpack plugins to do this work, place the output in static/js instead. Hugo will still see it and use it. Just be sure to modify the path where Hugo looks for the file in your search.html template.

Next, move themes/basic/assets/search.js to themes/basic/assets/js/index.js. This file will now become the entrypoint for Webpack:

```
$ mv themes/basic/assets/js/search.js themes/basic/assets/js/index.js
```

Open the file and import Axios and Lunr at the top of the file:

assets/portfolio/themes/basic/assets/js/index.js
```
'use strict'

➤  import axios from 'axios';
➤  import lunr from 'lunr';
```

Now integrate the file that Webpack will generate into your layout. Open themes/basic/layouts/_default/search.html and remove these lines, since Webpack is now loading and assembling the files:

```
{{ $lunr := resources.Get "js/lunr.js" }}
{{ $axios := resources.Get "js/axios.js" }}
{{ $search := resources.Get "js/search.js" }}
{{ $libs := slice $lunr $axios $search }}
```

Then modify the $js line so it only pulls in the app.js file that Webpack will generate:

assets/portfolio/themes/basic/layouts/_default/search.html
```
{{ $js := resources.Get "js/app.js" | minify | fingerprint }}
<script src="{{ $js.RelPermalink }}"></script>
```

Save the file.

You'll need to run Webpack to build the app.js file before you run the Hugo server. If you don't do this, Hugo will fail to build the site because it won't be able to find the app.js file in the assets folder.

Webpack is installed as a dependency of this project, rather than installed globally. To run it, you'd have to run the command node node_modules/webpack/bin/webpack.js. But since that's a lot to type, you can use the scripts section of package.json to create a shorter commmand.

Open the package.json file and locate the scripts section. As you learned earlier, this section lets you define scripts you want to run. You already have a build command which builds the site with Hugo. Add a new webpack command which runs webpack:

```
"scripts": {
  "build": "hugo --cleanDestinationDir",
  "hugo-server": "hugo server --disableFastRender",
  "webpack": "webpack"
  }
```

Be sure to add a comma to the end of the hugo-server line so that your JSON is valid.

Since you've added Webpack as a dependency of your project, you can use it in the scripts section without needing to specify its path.

You can now run npm run webpack to build the app.js file:

```
$ npm run webpack
> portfolio@1.0.0 webpack /Users/brianhogan/portfolio
> webpack

Hash: dbc9c6b673dd8cde7dd0
Version: webpack 4.41.2
Time: 315ms
Built at: 01/02/2020 8:45:15 PM
 Asset       Size  Chunks            Chunk Names
app.js  45.6 KiB       0  [emitted]  main
Entrypoint main = app.js
[11] ./themes/basic/assets/js/index.js 1.42 KiB {0} [built]
    + 28 hidden modules
```

Once Webpack completes, you can build the site or start the development server.

Hugo's development server watches files for changes, but it can't trigger external build tools like Webpack. You have two options at your disposal. The first option is to use two terminal windows. Have Hugo's server running in one window and run Webpack in the other window using its watch option. Add a new script to your package.json file named webpack-watch:

```
"scripts": {
  "build": "hugo --cleanDestinationDir",
  "hugo-server": "hugo server --disableFastRender",
  "webpack": "webpack",
  "webpack-watch": "webpack --watch",
},
```

Open a new terminal window and navigate to your project directory. Run npm run webpack-watch and it'll run, waiting for any changes to your files. When it sees changes, it will generate the new file. The Hugo dev server will then see the app.js file change, which will trigger a rebuild of the Hugo site.

Juggling two terminal windows isn't ideal, so you can create task that runs both servers in parallel using a single command. To do that, install the npm-run-all module, which lets you run multiple tasks in serial or parallel on all operating systems.

Install the module as a development dependency:

```
$ npm install --save-dev npm-run-all
```

Then create a new task called dev which runs Webpack and Hugo's servers:

```
"scripts": {
  "build": "hugo --cleanDestinationDir",
  "hugo-server": "hugo server --disableFastRender",
  "webpack": "webpack",
  "webpack-watch": "webpack --watch",
  "dev": "npm-run-all webpack --parallel webpack-watch hugo-server"
},
```

This new dev task runs Webpack by itself first to ensure that the app.js file is created. It then runs the webpack-watch and hugo-server tasks you defined.

Finally, the build task currently just builds the site with Hugo. Rename that task to hugo-build and add a new build task that runs Webpack and Hugo sequentially:

```
"build": "npm-run-all webpack hugo-build",
"hugo-build": "hugo --cleanDestinationDir",
```

You now have an integrated solution for using Webpack and Hugo together, as well as a build system.

Your Turn

You've explored several ways Hugo helps you manage your sites' assets. Try these additional exercises to practice these concepts:

1. Break your styles apart more by making the styles associated with project pages their own partial.

2. Use Sass variables to store your color values instead of hard-coding them throughout your stylesheets.

3. Read the Responsive Images[4] article on the Mozilla Developer Network site. Modify the postimage shortcode to implement the concepts in that article.

4. Now that you have Webpack working, explore using Vue or React for your search instead of vanilla JavaScript.

Wrapping Up

Hugo gives you everything you need to concatenate, minify, and fingerprint your styles and scripts. Now that you have incorporated these features into the site, your visitors will see faster download times, and you will ensure they will not be stuck with out-of-date versions of your styles and scripts when

---

4. https://developer.mozilla.org/en-US/docs/Learn/HTML/Multimedia_and_embedding/Responsive_images

you make future updates. Hugo's image manipulation functions, along with shortcodes, make managing assets much less complex, which means much less effort is required for you to create content with images. And when Hugo isn't enough, you now know how to integrate a Webpack-based workflow into your Hugo site.

There's a lot more you can do to your site, but you've tinkered enough for now; it's time to share it with the world. In the next chapter you'll look at a few options to deploy your site.

CHAPTER 8

Deploying the Site

Your site is ready for the world to see, and since everything Hugo produces is completely static content, the only requirement you have is an existing web server. At the most basic level, you can take the contents of the public directory and place them in your existing web server's web root directory.

However, copying the data directly to your web server isn't the only way to bring your site online quickly; there are other, more automated options. For example, you can use a script that automates pushing your code to a production server, you can use a hosting service with built-in continuous integration, you can transfer your site to cloud storage, or you can use containers to package your site into something you can deploy to a Docker host.

All of these options have their pros and cons. Ultimately, how you deploy your site depends entirely on what you have available—and because this book can't cover everything—this chapter will cover two specific scenarios and a more general approach.

You'll start by deploying your site to Netlify,[1] a service that hosts static websites. Netlify is a great option for people who don't have a background in deployment and want to get things running quickly and securely.

From there, you'll move on to deploying your site to Amazon's S3 cloud storage using Hugo's built-in deploy command. If you're already familiar with hosting static sites on S3, this is a fantastic option.

Finally, you'll look at deploying your site to more traditional web hosts like shared hosting providers, cloud servers, or your own internal servers.

---

1. https://netlify.com

Deploying to Netlify

Netlify is a commercial platform for hosting static websites and single page applications. To deploy to Netlify, you need to push your code to a remote Git repository. But first, you need to set up a local Git repository and get version control in place. Once that's done, you'll push your local repository to a remote repository so you can integrate it with other services.

If you don't have Git installed locally, follow the installation instructions on the official Git website.[2] Then, follow the instructions they provide to configure your client.[3]

Once Git is installed, navigate to your project directory and run the `git init` command to convert your directory into a new Git repository:

```
$ git init
```

Your Git repository should only contain the code and files for your site, which means you won't include the `node_modules` and `public` directories in your repository. You can specify files to ignore in a file named .gitignore.

Create a .gitignore file in the root of your project that excludes the following folders:

```
deploy/portfolio/.gitignore
# exclude JS dependencies
node_modules

# exclude Hugo's output
public
```

Save the .gitignore file, and then add the rest of the files to your repository:

```
$ git add .
```

This adds all of the files in the current directory and all child directories, except for those you've ignored.

> **Keep Hugo With Your Site**
>
> Since Hugo is a single binary, you could copy the Hugo executable to the root folder of your project and run it from there with ./hugo, ensuring you'll always have the version of Hugo you used to build your site. You could even check it in to version control so you can pull down everything you need later.

2.   https://git-scm.com/book/en/v2/Getting-Started-Installing-Git
3.   https://git-scm.com/book/en/v2/Getting-Started-First-Time-Git-Setup

At this point, you're ready to make your first commit:

```
$ git commit -m "initial import"
```

Although your files are committed locally, they won't be available on GitHub until you create a remote repository and push your code there. Visit GitHub, log in, and create a new repository named hugosite; however, don't create a .gitignore or README file in this repository. If you choose to create a public repository, remember that a public repository means everyone will be able to see all of the code you've built and how you built it. Sometimes you might want to keep that a secret, so you should use a private repository instead.

After you create the remote repository, add it to your local repository as a remote source so you can push your code:

```
$ git remote add origin git@github.com:your_username/hugosite.git
```

With the remote repository added, push your code to GitHub:

```
$ git push -u origin master
```

Now that your site is available, visit Netlify and log in with your GitHub account. Once logged in, choose New Site from Git. Under the Continuous Deployment section, select GitHub. Authorize Netlify to access your account.

Netlify will then inform you that it doesn't have access to any of your repositories. Click the Configure Netlify for GitHub button and give Netlify access to your hugosite repository.

Once you've configured the GitHub side of things, you'll return to Netlify's interface, and the hugosite repository displays in your list of repositories.

Select the hugosite repository to create your site and configure the deployment settings. Under the Basic Settings section, you'll configure the command to build your site:

Basic build settings

If you're using a static site generator or build tool, we'll need these settings to build your site.

Learn more in the docs ↗

Build command

npm run build

Publish directory

public

Show advanced

For the build command, enter npm run build, the command you created in Using Webpack and npm with Hugo, on page 102.

Select Advanced Settings and add an environment variable named HUGO_VERSION. Enter the version of Hugo you have installed on your local machine. If you are not sure what version you have, you can use the hugo version command to find out:

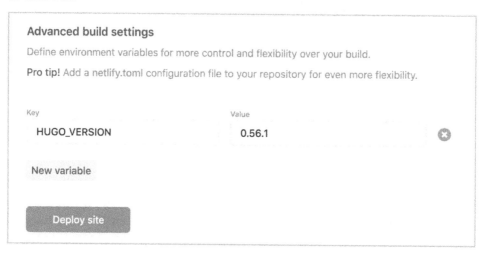

Press the Deploy Site button and wait while your site deploys. Netlify downloads the appropriate version of Hugo, installs the Node modules you specified in the package.json file, and runs your build command:

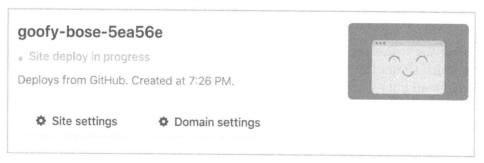

After a few minutes, you'll see the link to your site appear. To preview your site, follow the link.

You can point your own domain name to your site by following the instructions provided. Netlify will walk you through the process of purchasing a new domain or verifying an existing domain name. It will also walk you through securing your site with a TLS certificate from Let's Encrypt.[4]

After you select your domain and configure it to point to your Netlify site, you need to modify the baseURL setting for your site to match the domain name you've chosen. If you don't, the URLs for your RSS feeds and JSON feeds you included in your site's header won't work properly.

There are two ways in which you can modify the baseURL setting:

- Edit the baseURL field in the config.toml file.
- Alter the hugo build command to specify the base URL for the site.

To change the baseURL field in config.toml, open the file in your editor, and replace baseURL with your domain. Be sure to include the https:// and also leave a trailing slash at the end:

```
baseURL = "https://yourdomain.com/"
languageCode = "en-us"
title = "Brian's Portfolio"
```

After you make these changes, save the file and get ready to commit them and push them to GitHub.

First, add the config.toml file using the git add command. Next, use the git commit command with a commit message explaining the change you made. Finally, use the git push command to push the changes to your remote repository:

```
$ git add config.toml
$ git commit -m "Set the base URL for the site"
$ git push origin master
```

The other way to change the site's base URL is to modify the command that builds your site.

Open the package.json file in your editor and change the hugo-build script so that it uses the -b switch to specify the base URL:

```
"scripts": {
  "build": "npm-run-all webpack hugo-build",
  "hugo-build": "hugo --cleanDestinationDir -b https://yourdomain.com/",
```

Save this file, and then add the package.json file using the git add command, followed by the commit command to commit the changes, and the push command to push the changes to your remote repository:

---

4. https://letsencrypt.org

```
$ git add config.toml
$ git commit -m "Set the base URL for the site"
$ git push origin master
```

Because Netlify is watching your repository, it will notice this commit and trigger a new deploy. And since you've committed your code to GitHub, you can use all of the collaborative tools it offers. You can even create new posts using GitHub's interface, and Netlify will deploy those new pages for you.

Netlify gives you a fast and configurable way to deploy your static site. The free plan is good for small personal sites. However, as your site grows, so do your hosting costs.

Let's explore another way to deploy your site.

Deploying to Cloud Storage with Hugo

Hugo has built-in support for deploying your site to cloud storage provided by Amazon S3, Google Compute Storage, and Microsoft Azure. To use these services, you need to configure Hugo with the information it needs about where to place the files.

Let's configure Hugo to deploy to Amazon S3.

Before you start, you should be aware that this method will result in a site that doesn't have a custom domain and won't be secured with a TLS certificate. However, you can combine this approach with Amazon's Cloudfront[5] and Route 53[6] services to configure TLS certificates and a domain name for your site. As such, this approach is targeted toward people who have some experience hosting static content on S3.

To use Hugo to deploy to S3, you need an AWS account. If you don't have an account, visit the AWS site [7] to set one up.

You also need an AWS access key. To set this up, follow Amazon's documentation.[8] Make sure to record your access key and the accompanying secret. You won't be able to retrieve the secret once you create it, so if you lose it, you'll have to generate a new access key and secret.

---

5.   https://aws.amazon.com/cloudfront/

6.   https://aws.amazon.com/route53/

7.   https://aws.amazon.com/

8.   https://aws.amazon.com/premiumsupport/knowledge-center/create-access-key/

Keep Your AWS Credentials Safe!

 If you're not careful and someone else gets a hold of your AWS access key, they can use it to access your account, spin up resources, and spend a lot of your money. Keep your access keys safe, and do not store them in version control systems.

Next, you need to download and install the AWS command-line utility.[9] You'll use this utility to create a local configuration file that stores your AWS credentials.

Once you've installed the CLI, configure your credentials with the AWS CLI using the following command:

```
$ aws configure
```

The tool prompts you for your AWS acces key and secret for your account. Enter both, then accept the default values for the rest of the prompts. This process creates a file in your home directory that contains your AWS credentials. The aws CLI app uses this file to find credentials when you run commands, and Hugo uses this file to make its connection to your S3 bucket when you tell it to deploy your site.

To host a website on S3, you need to create a bucket for your site, configure the bucket to serve web content, and apply a policy that lets people view all of the bucket's contents. Although you can do this through the AWS console, it's much quicker to use the AWS CLI tool.

Create the S3 bucket using the following command, but use your own name for your bucket, as bucket names must be unique:

```
$ aws s3api create-bucket --bucket bph-pp-hugoprod \
      --acl public-read --region us-east-1
```

This command creates the bucket bph-pp-hugo-prod in the US East 1 AWS region.

To use an S3 bucket as a website, you have to enable it to serve web pages and define the index document. You can also define the name of the error document you want to use, but this is optional:

```
$ aws s3 website s3://bph-pp-hugoprod/ \
      --index-document index.html \
      --error-document error.html
```

You're ready to create a *bucket policy* that allows access to your bucket. Without this policy, people won't be able to view your content.

---

9. https://docs.aws.amazon.com/cli/latest/userguide/install-bundle.html

First, create the policy as a JSON file named bucketpolicy.json with the following contents:

deploy/portfolio/bucketpolicy.json

```
{
  "Version":"2012-10-17",
  "Statement":[
    {
            "Sid":"PublicReadGetObject",
        "Effect":"Allow",
            "Principal": "*",
        "Action": ["s3:GetObject"],
        "Resource": ["arn:aws:s3:::bph-pp-hugoprod/*"]
    }
  ]
}
```

Then, use the aws s3api command to apply the policy to the bucket:

```
aws s3api put-bucket-policy --bucket bph-pp-hugoprod \
        --policy file://bucketpolicy.json
```

Your bucket is now configured to serve a static website. Not only can you use the aws command to sync the files to the bucket, you can also use the hugo deploy command to transfer the files, giving you some additional options.

Open Hugo's config.toml file and add a new deployments section that specifies the bucket and region like this:

deploy/portfolio/config.toml

```
[deployment]

  [[deployment.targets]]
  name = "prod"
  URL = "s3://bph-pp-hugoprod?region=us-east-1"
```

You can create multiple deployment targets for your site. For example, you can have a staging target which publishes to one bucket and a production target that publishes to another.

To increase your site's performance, you can compress your scripts, pages, and styles so they'll download faster. Add this section to the file:

deploy/portfolio/config.toml

```
[[deployment.matchers]]
pattern = "^.+\\.(html|xml|js|css)$"
gzip = true
```

Save the file, and build your Hugo site again using the hugo --cleanDestinationDir command to ensure that the public folder is completely cleaned out and no artifacts from previous builds remain:

```
$ hugo --cleanDestinationDir
```

Now, use the hugo deploy command to upload the files to your bucket.

```
$ hugo deploy
```

Your site is now live. To access it, visit the URL associated with your bucket. In this example, the URL is http://bph-pp-hugoprod.s3-website.us-east-1.amazonaws.com.

In Using Webpack and npm with Hugo, on page 102, you created a package.json file that had some build tasks defined. Modify that package.json file and add a hugo-deploy command for deploying the site, as well as a deploy command which does the entire build and deploy process:

```
"scripts": {
  "build": "npm-run-all webpack hugo-build",
  "hugo-build": "hugo --cleanDestinationDir",
  "webpack": "webpack",
  "webpack-watch": "webpack --watch",
  "hugo-deploy": "hugo deploy",
  "deploy": "npm-run-all build hugo-deploy"
  "dev": "npm-run-all webpack --parallel webpack-watch hugo-server"
},
```

The next time you're ready to deploy your site, run the command npm run deploy. Your site builds and deploys to S3 with a single command.

At this point, you're ready to explore using Cloudfront and Route 53 to point your own domain at the site. Once you've done that, you need to modify the base URL for your Hugo site to reflect the domain. The easiest way to do that is to change the hugo-build task in your package.json file to specify the base URL:

```
"scripts": {
  "build": "npm-run-all webpack hugo-build",
  "hugo-build": "hugo --cleanDestinationDir -b https://yourdomain.com/",
  "webpack": "webpack",
```

Save the file and run the npm run deploy to rebuild and redeploy the site.

The steps in this section are similar for other cloud providers. The only major difference is the value you use for the URL field in config.toml. If you're using Google, specify your bucket name like this:

```
URL = "gs://your_bucket_name"
```

If you're using Azure, specify the blob:

```
URL = "azblob://$your_blob_name"
```

Consult the instructions for your cloud provider on how to configure the resources and access permissions, and how to connect your domain name to those resources.

If you're not interested in using cloud storage, you can deploy Hugo to a standard web server.

Deploying to a Traditional Web Server

Deploying your Hugo site to a traditional web server is no different than transferring web pages you've made by hand. You use Hugo to generate your site and copy the contents of the public directory to your server's default web root.

Before you get started, you need the following information:

- The host name or IP address of your server

- The user account to use

- The password for the user (unless you've set up public key authentication)

- The path to the directory on the remote server where you want to store your files

- The fully qualified domain name for your site

Your site should also have SFTP or *shell access* enabled. SFTP is a secure method of transferring files to remote servers. Shell access means you can log in to the remote server using the ssh command. If you have shell access, you can use the scp command, short for secure copy, to transfer your files, or the rsync program to synchronize the contents of your public directory to your web server.

If you're working with a cloud server, VPS, or a local Linux or BSD-based server running Ubuntu, Debian, Red Hat Enterprise Linux, FreeBSD, or other Linux distributions, you most likely have shell access enabled. Some shared hosts provide *shell access* as well, although you may have to configure this or ask their support teams to enable it for you.

Once you have all of the information you need, you can do your first deployment. First, modify config.toml to specify the base URL for your site, changing it from example.org to your domain:

```
baseURL = "https://yourdomain.com/"
languageCode = "en-us"
title = "Brian's Portfolio"
```

Save the file, and prepare for its transfer. To transfer the files to your server, you can either use a graphical SFTP program like FileZilla[10] or some command-line tools.

With something like FileZilla, you'd plug your credentials into the app and then transfer the contents of your Hugo site's public directory to the directory on your shared host.

Using the command-line interface on macOS or Linux machines, if the sftp command is available, and you wanted to transfer the public directory from your Hugo site to your web host's public_html directory, you'd do it like this:

```
$ sftp -r username@hostname:public_html <<< 'put public/*'
```

If you have shell access to your server, you can use the scp command to transfer your files securely. The following command transfers the contents of the public directory to the public_html directory on the remote server:

```
$ scp -r public/* username@hostname:public_html
```

With scp, you first specify the source files, then the destination. The -r switch recursively copies files and directories.

You can also use the rsync command to transfer files to your server. With rsync, you can synchronize the contents of your local directory with another directory, and even compress the files so they'll transfer faster. The following command uses rsync to connect to your remote server, copy the contents of the public directory to your server's public_html directory, and remove any files on the server that aren't in your local directory:

```
$ rsync -avz --delete public/ username@hostname.com:public_html
```

The -a switch tells rsync to use "archive mode", which recursively selects all files and makes a complete backup, preserving permissions and times. The -v switch shows verbose output, and the -z switch compresses the files.

If you've manually placed files on your server, the rsync command will delete those files if it doesn't find them in your local public directory, so you should ensure that this command is the only way files get on your server.

In Using Webpack and npm with Hugo, on page 102, you defined some tasks that made building your site easier. Modify your package.json file to include the rsync command to deploy your site, and then make a master deploy command that builds and uploads your files:

---

10. https://filezilla-project.org/

```
"scripts": {
  "build": "npm-run-all webpack hugo-build",
  "hugo-build": "hugo --cleanDestinationDir",
  "webpack": "node_modules/webpack/bin/webpack.js",
  "webpack-watch": "node_modules/webpack/bin/webpack.js --watch",
  "upload": "rsync -avz --delete public/ username@hostname.com:public_html",
  "deploy": "npm-run-all webpack hugo-build upload",
  "dev": "npm-run-all webpack --parallel webpack-watch hugo-server"
},
```

Be sure to change the username, hostname, and remote path to match the values for your own site.

With these changes in place, you can run npm run deploy to build and upload your site to your server.

> **Joe asks:**
> # What If I Don't Have a Server?
>
> If you don't have an existing web server, you can set one up yourself or use a *shared hosting provider.*
>
> Shared hosting providers are low-cost platforms that give you some space on a server to host your web pages. You point your domain name to one of their servers and they serve up the pages. Shared hosting is one of the most common ways people host personal and small business sites. Dreamhost[a] is a well-known shared hosting provider that's inexpensive and offers SFTP and shell access so you can automate your deployments.
>
> On a shared host, you share resources with hundreds, or thousands, of other accounts, and you have very little control over how the web servers are configured. If you want more control, you can set up your own dedicated server, or use a cloud server provided by DigitalOcean,[b] Linode,[c] Amazon AWS,[d] Microsoft Azure,[e] or Google Cloud.[f] Unlike a shared host, you're responsible for managing the operating system and the web server software. Each provider has documentation on how to set up and secure your web server.
>
> The deployment process itself is identical whether you're using a shared host or your own server.
>
> ---
>
> a. https://dreamhost.com
> b. https://digitalocean.com
> c. https://linode.com
> d. https://aws.amazon.com
> e. https://azure.microsoft.com
> f. https://cloud.google.com

Your Turn

There are a few other methods you can explore when it comes to deploying your site:

1. Explore how to deploy your site to GitHub Pages.[11]

2. Explore GitHub Actions[12] and use it to run your deployment commands when files in your repository change.

3. Explore NetlifyCMS,[13] an open source frontend for managing your content and deploying changes.

Wrapping Up

As you've seen in this chapter, there are many ways to deploy your Hugo site to production, and the method you choose depends on your specific situation. Deploying to Netlify is a great way to get a personal site online quickly, while deploying to your own web server might be the only option you have for your company docs site.

You've used Hugo to build a small, but feature-packed personal site. You've created your own theme from scratch; added content sections; served your content as JSON and RSS; consumed data from other sources; built a blog with comments; managed images, CSS, and scripts; added a search feature; and explored several ways to deploy your Hugo site to production and share it with the world. With this foundation, you're ready to explore the various other features Hugo provides.

Hugo is an open source project under active development. As you learn more, consider joining the community. Ask and answer questions in the Hugo Community,[14] build a theme and share it on the Hugo Themes site,[15] or contribute directly to the project itself with bug reports, documentation updates, or pull requests that fix outstanding issues.

---

11. https://pages.github.com/
12. https://github.com/features/actions
13. https://www.netlifycms.org/
14. https://discourse.gohugo.io/
15. https://themes.gohugo.io/

Migrating to Hugo

Now that you know how Hugo works, you're probably thinking, "OK, how can I move my existing content to Hugo?" In a perfect world, you'd simply put your content in Hugo's content directory as Markdown files and everything would just work. However, we don't live in a perfect world, and it often ends up being a little more nuanced than that.

Depending on how your content is organized and what additions or plugins you've added to your existing system, the migration could take anywhere from a few hours to a few months to complete.

In this chapter, you'll review the migration process at a high level, which will help you plan and map out what you need for your own migration plan.

Understanding What You Have

Before you start any migration, it's best to fully understand what you're migrating. How much content do you have? What type of content is it, and is it properly tagged? Are there any broken links? What features of the existing site do you plan to keep?

When doing any migration, it's best to clean up the source material before starting. This is especially true with older WordPress sites that have undergone multiple database migrations. Regardless of your current website delivery system, here's a short-list of things to investigate and address before attempting your migration:

1. Verify that all of your content is tagged and categorized.

2. Ensure the author information is consistent across all pages.

3. Check for content consistency. Look for mixes of UTF-8, Latin, and ASCII characters like curly quotes and straight quotes. Be aware that older

posts might not use the correct encoding; if you fix these now, it'll save you time later.

4.   Clean out any drafts or previous versions that you don't need.

5.   Fix broken links. Most blog platforms and content management systems have this capability built in or offer a plugin to help.

6.   Take inventory of any server-side scripts your site uses, like widgets, image galleries, and other plugins.

Do a thorough audit of your site. It's almost like moving to a new house or apartment; pack everything up nicely before you begin the move.

Once you have an idea of what you have, and you know everything is in good shape, you're ready to start moving your content.

Transferring the Content

The most challenging part of any migration is extracting the content from the existing site and getting it presentable in a format the new site can use. Thankfully, with Hugo's rising popularity, there are a few tools and scripts available that handle a lot of the heavy lifting for you. But how you do it depends on which platform you're migrating from.

If you're migrating from a WordPress blog, you can use the WordPress-to-Hugo Export plugin.[1] This plugin exports all of your content, placing each post in its own Markdown file. The plugin preserves the original post's permalink, and places it in the front matter section of the corresponding Markdown file. It also stores the draft status.

If you have a self-hosted WordPress installation, you can install the WordPress-to-Hugo Export plugin and use it from within the WordPress user interface. Download the plugin, extract it, and upload it to your server via SFTP or SCP into your site's /wp-content/plugins/ directory. Then, visit your site, log in as an admin, and select Export to Hugo from the Tools menu.

If your WordPress site is hosted on WordPress.com, or you don't have direct access to the server, things will be more difficult. You'll need to set up a local WordPress instance, export the data from your existing site as an XML file, import your data into your local WordPress instance, and then install and use the plugin.

---

1.   https://github.com/SchumacherFM/wordpress-to-hugo-exporter

If you're using Jekyll as your current platform, Hugo has a built-in command to migrate your content. Ensure you have all of the source files for your Jekyll site and use the following command to convert your content:

```
$ hugo import jekyll jekyll_root_path target_path
```

If you're using Ghost, Tumblr, or other platforms, Hugo has a list of tools and scripts[2] you can use to help you get your content out.

Whichever method you use to migrate your content, remember that search engines and other sites may be pointing to your content, so you want to make sure that those links still work after your migration. Use the url field in front matter to specify the URL you want to use, or configure your web server to redirect visitors to the new URLs. If you're using Netlify, you can use their support for redirects.[3]

Automated scripts will get you about 80% of the way there. Depending on how your original system stored your content, the translation to Markdown might not be as smooth as you'd hoped. Many of the conversion utilities attempt to convert HTML content to Markdown. If your content has HTML that can't be converted, the conversion process might leave the HTML alone, leaving you with a mix of HTML and Markdown. Hugo's Markdown renderer will ignore HTML and JavaScript in Markdown documents. You may have to manually clean up the content yourself file by file. It can be a chore, but if you take the time to do that cleanup, all of your content will be clean, in plain-text Markdown documents, and will be much easier to manage going forward.

If you have some complex HTML in your content, and you can't figure out how to convert it, or don't like the results, you can configure Hugo's Markdown renderer to operate in "unsafe" mode, which will allow Hugo to render the HTML fragments. Add the following code to your config.toml file:

```
[markup]
  [markup.goldmark]
    [markup.goldmark.renderer]
      unsafe = true
```

This will let you get more of your content migrated, but it does open a potential security hole that would allow unsafe code to run. For example, if you'd migrated some code from a WordPress site, and one of your pages had some malicious JavaScript code on it that you didn't notice, Hugo's defaults

---

2.   https://gohugo.io/tools/migrations/
3.   https://docs.netlify.com/routing/redirects/

would prevent that malicious code from rendering. So, before turning this on, triple-check your content.

If you're not willing to do all of that cleanup work, you have two options: you can leave your content as-is and fix it over time, or you can unpublish the content.

To unpublish content, do a global search and replace and set the draft status of everything before a certain date to true, so it will no longer be published. When you put things in a draft status, you can update them over time, and reactivate them when you're ready. This will likely break external links to your content, so be mindful of that. As an alternative, you can add a new field to your front matter and modify your template to show a deprecation notice or other disclaimer for pages with that field.

Automation Only Gets You So Far

A WordPress site I recently imported had over 17 years of posts, and the first three years of posts were originally on a different blogging platform entirely. These posts were done in HTML tables and didn't have titles. I was able to import all of the content, but when I reviewed some of the pages in the browser, elements were missing. Some of the HTML couldn't be converted to Markdown.

I had to review each Markdown file, add an appropriate title for the pages, and clean up the code. It was a tedious process, and I did decide that some content couldn't be moved right away. For those pieces, I added a notice to those pages letting the reader know that there's still some work in progress, as I didn't want to break any incoming links from Google by unpublishing the content.

Your pages and posts aren't the only bits of content you'll need to think about.

Handling Comments

If you have a vibrant community of people sharing their thoughts and opinions on your content, you will likely want to keep that content on your new site as well.

The best approach to keep your comments is to migrate them to Disqus directly when possible. Disqus has guides for importing comments[4] that you can refer to for help with this process.

Some of the export scripts can preserve comments as well. You can then freeze those old comments on those posts to prevent future commenting.

---

4.   https://help.disqus.com/en/collections/191709-import-export-and-syncing

You might consider a combination of these approaches too. For example, you might migrate your most recent posts' comments to Disqus, while treating anything over a year old as an archive.

Handling Images and Other Assets

Images need to be migrated from your old site to your new site, just like content, and how you migrate them depends entirely on how your images were linked to your content. If you hosted your images on an asset server with absolute links, then there's nothing you'll need to do, as the links will still work. If your site images were uploaded through your CMS, the links in the content pages may need some updates depending on where those images are located now.

Watch Out for Inconsistent URLs

One site I migrated had inconsistent references to images in the content. About half of the references in the site used images/ instead of /images/ as the base URL. It's such a subtle difference that it took me a lot longer than I care to admit to notice the actual problem. A quick find-and-replace later and it was all sorted out. But you're going to want to audit your images, and you should see if you can fix them before you migrate.

The WordPress export plugin for Hugo places all of the images in the static folder. If you have a lot of images, this can get messy. You may want to spend some time organizing the content and updating any image references.

If you were using an image gallery plugin that relies on server-side processing, like one written in PHP, it won't work with a Hugo site. You could use a JavaScript-based library, but you can also create your own image gallery using a Hugo shortcode that reads files from your static folder and constructs a link and image for each one.

Create a file in your theme named shortcodes/gallery.html with the following contents:

```
{{ $path := .Get 0 }}
{{ $files := readDir (print "/static/" $path) }}

<div class="gallery">
  {{ range $files }}
  <a href="{{ $path }}/{{ .Name }}">
    <img src="{{ $path }}/{{ .Name }}">
  </a>
  {{ end }}
</div>
```

This fetches all files from a given directory, iterates over each one, and displays them on the page.

You can then add some CSS to style each image in the gallery:

```
.gallery img {
  margin: 1em;
  height: 240px;
  width: 320px;
}
```

Invoke the gallery by adding the shortcode to a content page:

```
{{< gallery "/images/vacation-photos" >}}
```

In this example, the gallery displays all the images located in static/images/vacation-photos.

This approach uses CSS to resize the images, which isn't ideal. You could use what you learned in Using a Shortcode to Process Images, on page 99 to build a more robust version of this that reads images from a page bundle and resizes them, creating smaller thumbnails.

You can use custom shortcodes to migrate many features from your current site, from video and code embeds to social sharing widgets.

Your existing site may have other files, like PDF documents, downloadable files, or other assets. Moving those to their own asset server will make your site easier to manage, but you can also create folders in the static/ folder just like you would with images. If you re-create the same directory structure as the original site, your files will be accesible using the same URLs.

Checking Links

Images, hyperlinks, and other references might not entirely survive a migration, and spot-checking everything is time-consuming. The Broken Link Checker[5] command-line tool can help identify these issues quickly. It requires Node.js, but if you're doing web work, you probably already have that.

Install the tool globally:

```
$ npm install broken-link-checker -g
```

Then, run the hugo server command to launch your site.

---

5. https://github.com/stevenvachon/broken-link-checker

After the site launches, run the `blc` command to recursively scan your Hugo site and let it show you what's wrong:

```
$ blc http://localhost:1313 -r -o
```

The `-o` switch tells `blc` to order the results so it's easier to fix any issues. The `-r` switch tells the system to do a recursive scan.

Fix any broken links, and rescan your system until you don't find new ones, as the previously broken links might lead to pages that have broken links of their own.

Once you have the content in a good state, you'll want to replicate your theme.

Replicating the Theme

You learned how to build a theme in this book, so you should have all of the tools you need to duplicate your existing theme, which is mostly a manual task. You'll use `hugo new theme` to create a new theme, copy over your stylesheets and place them in the `assets` folder of your theme, create new partials, and create the appropriate templates for your content sections. Move over any tracking or analytics code you've integrated into your theme as well.

The basic theme you created in this book is a good starting point. Use that as the base and apply your changes over the top.

You might not be able to bring everything over from your old theme. Some platforms have additional features in their themes beyond colors and content placement. For example, WordPress sites often have an "archives" section where you can create pages that list posts by year and month. You might consider writing some code to generate those layout pages, or use the tagging approach used in Organizing Content with Taxonomies, on page 58 to build those pages.

In addition, your theme may have extra widgets you're relying on, many written in a back-end programming language like PHP. If you're moving your site, you'll have to take inventory of those widgets, determine which ones you want to carry forward, and then decide on replacements. For instance, if you're using a Twitter plugin to display your most recent tweets, you might consider using Twitter's official JavaScript widget on your site.[6]

Your site is migrated, you've re-created your theme and tested everything; it's time to cut over to the new site.

---

6. https://publish.twitter.com/

Making the Switch

The safest method for deploying your new site to production is to deploy it to a different server and change your domain name's DNS settings to point to the new server instead of the old one. That way you still have access to the old site in production in case you need something.

Deploy your site using one of the methods in Chapter 8, Deploying the Site, on page 109. Then, once you've tested the site, update your DNS settings for your domain to point to the new site. It will take anywhere from a few hours to a couple of days for the DNS changes to propagate around the world. You can use WhatsMyDNS[7] to track your DNS changes.

Once your site's up, ensure existing links to your site work too. Search for your content on Google and follow the inbound links to ensure people can find your documents. If the links are broken, address those quickly with redirects or by altering the url field in the appropriate page's front matter. Redeploy the site and check the links again.

When you're confident things are completely migrated, you can back up your old site and decommission it.

Wrapping Up

When you're moving a site from one platform to another, there are many things to consider, from how to transfer your content to how to replace the existing site with the migrated one. This appendix provided a high-level overview, but it may not have covered all of the areas your site will need to consider. Your migration will take time and you may encounter some places where you'll have to get creative. However, when you're done, you'll have your content in plain-text Markdown, nicely organized, making it ready for whatever the future holds.

---

7. https://www.whatsmydns.net/

Bibliography

[Hog19]   Brian P. Hogan. *Small, Sharp Software Tools*. The Pragmatic Bookshelf, Raleigh, NC, 2019.

Thank you!

How did you enjoy this book? Please let us know. Take a moment and email us at support@pragprog.com with your feedback. Tell us your story and you could win free ebooks. Please use the subject line "Book Feedback."

Ready for your next great Pragmatic Bookshelf book? Come on over to https://pragprog.com and use the coupon code BUYANOTHER2020 to save 30% on your next ebook.

Void where prohibited, restricted, or otherwise unwelcome. Do not use ebooks near water. If rash persists, see a doctor. Doesn't apply to *The Pragmatic Programmer* ebook because it's older than the Pragmatic Bookshelf itself. Side effects may include increased knowledge and skill, increased marketability, and deep satisfaction. Increase dosage regularly.

And thank you for your continued support,

Andy Hunt, Publisher

Small, Sharp Software Tools

The command-line interface is making a comeback. That's because developers know that all the best features of your operating system are hidden behind a user interface designed to help average people use the computer. But you're not the average user, and the CLI is the most efficient way to get work done fast. Turn tedious chores into quick tasks: read and write files, manage complex directory hierarchies, perform network diagnostics, download files, work with APIs, and combine individual programs to create your own workflows. Put down that mouse, open the CLI, and take control of your software development environment.

Brian P. Hogan

(326 pages) ISBN: 9781680502961. $38.95

https://pragprog.com/book/bhcldev

tmux 2

Your mouse is slowing you down. The time you spend context switching between your editor and your consoles eats away at your productivity. Take control of your environment with tmux, a terminal multiplexer that you can tailor to your workflow. With this updated second edition for tmux 2.3, you'll customize, script, and leverage tmux's unique abilities to craft a productive terminal environment that lets you keep your fingers on your keyboard's home row.

Brian P. Hogan

(102 pages) ISBN: 9781680502213. $21.95

https://pragprog.com/book/bhtmux2

React for Real

When traditional web development techniques don't cut it, try React. Use React to create highly interactive web pages faster and with fewer errors. With a little JavaScript experience under your belt, you'll be up and running in no time creating dynamic web applications. Craft isolated components that make your apps easier to develop and maintain, with plenty of guidance on best practices. Set up automated tests, and make pages render fast for your users. See how to use your React skills to integrate with other front-end technologies when needed.

Ludovico Fischer
(118 pages) ISBN: 9781680502633. $26.95
https://pragprog.com/book/lfreact

Practical Microservices

MVC and CRUD make software easier to write, but harder to change. Microservice-based architectures can help even the smallest of projects remain agile in the long term, but most tutorials meander in theory or completely miss the point of what it means to be microservice based. Roll up your sleeves with real projects and learn the most important concepts of evented architectures. You'll have your own deployable, testable project and a direction for where to go next.

Ethan Garofolo
(290 pages) ISBN: 9781680506457. $45.95
https://pragprog.com/book/egmicro

Real-Time Phoenix

Give users the real-time experience they expect, by using Elixir and Phoenix Channels to build applications that instantly react to changes and reflect the application's true state. Learn how Elixir and Phoenix make it easy and enjoyable to create real-time applications that scale to a large number of users. Apply system design and development best practices to create applications that are easy to maintain. Gain confidence by learning how to break your applications before your users do. Deploy applications with minimized resource use and maximized performance.

Stephen Bussey
(326 pages) ISBN: 9781680507195. $45.95
https://pragprog.com/book/sbsockets

Programming Machine Learning

You've decided to tackle machine learning — because you're job hunting, embarking on a new project, or just think self-driving cars are cool. But where to start? It's easy to be intimidated, even as a software developer. The good news is that it doesn't have to be that hard. Master machine learning by writing code one line at a time, from simple learning programs all the way to a true deep learning system. Tackle the hard topics by breaking them down so they're easier to understand, and build your confidence by getting your hands dirty.

Paolo Perrotta
(340 pages) ISBN: 9781680506600. $47.95
https://pragprog.com/book/pplearn

Competing with Unicorns

Today's tech unicorns develop software differently. They've developed a way of working that lets them scale like an enterprise while working like a startup. These techniques can be learned. This book takes you behind the scenes and shows you how companies like Google, Facebook, and Spotify do it. Leverage their insights, so your teams can work better together, ship higher-quality product faster, innovate more quickly, and compete with the unicorns.

Jonathan Rasmusson
(138 pages) ISBN: 9781680507232. $26.95
https://pragprog.com/book/jragile

Programming Flutter

Develop your next app with Flutter and deliver native look, feel, and performance on both iOS and Android from a single code base. Bring along your favorite libraries and existing code from Java, Kotlin, Objective-C, and Swift, so you don't have to start over from scratch. Write your next app in one language, and build it for both Android and iOS. Deliver the native look, feel, and performance you and your users expect from an app written with each platform's own tools and languages. Deliver apps fast, doing half the work you were doing before and exploiting powerful new features to speed up development. Write once, run anywhere.

Carmine Zaccagnino
(368 pages) ISBN: 9781680506952. $47.95
https://pragprog.com/book/czflutr

The Pragmatic Bookshelf

The Pragmatic Bookshelf features books written by professional developers for professional developers. The titles continue the well-known Pragmatic Programmer style and continue to garner awards and rave reviews. As development gets more and more difficult, the Pragmatic Programmers will be there with more titles and products to help you stay on top of your game.

Visit Us Online

This Book's Home Page
https://pragprog.com/book/bhhugo
Source code from this book, errata, and other resources. Come give us feedback, too!

Keep Up to Date
https://pragprog.com
Join our announcement mailing list (low volume) or follow us on twitter @pragprog for new titles, sales, coupons, hot tips, and more.

New and Noteworthy
https://pragprog.com/news
Check out the latest pragmatic developments, new titles and other offerings.

Save on the ebook

Save on the ebook versions of this title. Owning the paper version of this book entitles you to purchase the electronic versions at a terrific discount.

PDFs are great for carrying around on your laptop—they are hyperlinked, have color, and are fully searchable. Most titles are also available for the iPhone and iPod touch, Amazon Kindle, and other popular e-book readers.

Buy now at *https://pragprog.com/coupon*

Contact Us

Online Orders: *https://pragprog.com/catalog*
Customer Service: *support@pragprog.com*
International Rights: *translations@pragprog.com*
Academic Use: *academic@pragprog.com*
Write for Us: *http://write-for-us.pragprog.com*
Or Call: +1 800-699-7764